THE WINTERTHUR GUIDE TO

COLOR
in Your
GARDEN

Plant Combinations and Practical Advice
from the Winterthur Garden

Ruth N. Joyce

A Winterthur Book
Distributed by University Press of New England

The printing of this book was made possible, in part, by the generosity of the Friends of Winterthur.

Editor: Mary Ellen Wilson
Designer: Lemonides Design Group
Photography: Ruth N. Joyce

Library of Congress Cataloging-in-Publication Data

Joyce, Ruth, 1927-
    The Winterthur guide to color in your garden : plant combinations and practical advice
    from the Winterthur Garden / Ruth Joyce.
       p. cm. -- (A Winterthur book)
    Includes bibliographical references and index.
    ISBN 0-912724-62-5 (pbk. : alk. paper)
    1. Color in gardening. 2. Landscape plants. 3. Henry Francis du Pont Winterthur Museum Gardens (Del.)
    I. Henry Francis du Pont Winterthur Museum. II. Title.
    SB454.3.C64J69 2004
    635.9'68--dc22   2003025727

To all who have helped

preserve this extraordinary creation,

the Winterthur Garden.

Contents

Foreword

Henry Francis du Pont was a man of vision, and the extraordinary landscape at Winterthur forms part of his remarkable legacy. Du Pont's jewel of a garden, an unsurpassed collection of American art and antiques, and a world-renowned library and research center constitute the "crown" that is Winterthur, an American country estate.

The history of this unique national treasure dates from 1839, when Jacques Antoine and Evelina du Pont Bidermann built the first house here and named the property Winterthur, after Bidermann's ancestral home in Switzerland. Henry Francis du Pont, the last private resident, brought the estate to its glory in the early twentieth century and founded Winterthur Museum in 1951. Today this former du Pont family home comprises nearly 1,000 acres nestled in Delaware's scenic Brandywine Valley.

H. F. du Pont relied on the art of horticulture and landscape design to transform his beloved countryside into a magical, romantic world set apart. A true gardener, he spent countless hours diligently noting details of his planting schemes, from flower color and plant habit to bloom time and care. He continually experimented with plant combinations and placement to create a natural-looking garden that belies such careful planning. Clearly his painstaking efforts triumphed. The Winterthur Garden is now considered to be one of the finest examples of succession of bloom. Indeed, the cheerful emergence of earliest bulbs on March Bank, the magnificent tapestry of blossoms in Azalea Woods, the vibrancy of late-summer wildflowers, and the festive holly trees of winter months make every visit special—an offering of enjoyable surprises and welcome pleasures.

We invite you to read about H. F. du Pont's design principles and plant groupings in the following pages. They will surely entice you to experiment in your own garden. We hope, too, that you will visit Winterthur and be a guest in ours. Experience the gently rolling hills, inviting meadows, and serene woodlands that delight the senses and impart tranquility in all seasons. Du Pont envisioned the creation of a country place museum that future generations would learn from and enjoy. His success is truly our reward.

Leslie Greene Bowman
Director
Winterthur, An American Country Estate

The Winterthur estate includes ponds, streams, fields, and meadows whose natural beauty appeals to all.

Preface

My father, Henry Francis du Pont, would have found this book enchanting. Set within his family home—which through good fortune, hard work, and perhaps a touch of genius he made still more beautiful—it incorporates characteristics intrinsic to his own makeup: the aesthetic, the scholarly, the practical.

The Winterthur Guide to Color in Your Garden provides a superb gardener's manual that invites us into exciting garden spaces, whether vast or intimate, open or woodland. It also introduces us to exotic diversity, for the plants described in the following pages come from all over the world, including eight Asian and four European countries as well as Africa and the Americas.

The chapters are divided into two sections: an introduction to a particular garden setting, followed by invaluable notes for the home gardener, which include specific descriptions of plants, detailed instructions for growing them, and suggestions about how they might find a place in our more modest surroundings. "Gardening Basics" provides basic information about planting procedures as well as information about how Winterthur horticulturists implement them.

As the title indicates, the subject of color, which my father believed to be the key to every planting scheme, predominates here. Author Ruth Joyce writes evocatively about the white flowers of spring snowflake that "look like ballerina skirts"; the lavender and silvery petals and orange centers of an early crocus; the many-hued hellebore blossoms in ivory, ivory speckled with mauve, or deep purple to greenish; and the misty pink of a cherry tree that resembles "confetti caught in the air."

Another characteristic of this book, and one also shared by my father, is its tone of optimism. The words "dependable," "adaptable," and "relatively problem free" appear with encouraging frequency, and Ruth Joyce notes many trees, shrubs, and ground covers with these attributes.

This book would have captivated Henry Francis du Pont. Following a family tradition of furthering horticulture, my father delighted in sharing his beautiful home and garden, which he ultimately opened to the public. *The Winterthur Guide to Color in Your Garden* carries this concept still further, for it makes accessible to the home gardener the many garden plans and recesses of the Winterthur landscape, which my father knew and loved so intimately.

Ruth du Pont Lord Holmes

"I have always loved flowers and had a garden as a child ... and if you have grown up with flowers and really seen them you can't help [but] to have unconsciously absorbed an appreciation of proportion, color, detail, and material," H. F. du Pont, 1962.

Acknowledgments

With fondness, I remember all the friends and colleagues who have generously helped in the preparation of this book. My dear friend and mentor, Denise Magnani, whose concept the book was, has encouraged me throughout. Ruth Lord, another treasured friend, greeted the idea with enthusiasm, made valuable suggestions, and has honored the work with a charming preface. Thomas Buchter and John Feliciani contributed many worthy thoughts. Linda Eirhart cheerfully answered my countless questions about species and cultivars and checked the manuscript with care. The knowledgeable horticulture staff at Winterthur—Robert Billingham, David Birk, Susan Boss, Marlin Dise, Leigh Dungey, Randal Fisher, Suzanne French, Frank Lennox, Carol Long, Elizabeth Mazzio, Nadja McCormick, Steve Melton, Emilio Oliva, Brian Phiel, James Pirhalla, Robert Plankinton, W. Franklin Quinnette, John Salata, Scott Simpson, James M. Smith Jr., and Kevin Stouts—freely shared their secrets of success and ferreted out mistakes in the early text.

Alberta Melloy, Patricia Pleva, and Jonathan Kissell were instrumental in making the forcing-branches section a reality. Linda Barry was ever helpful. Special thanks to my children and their spouses, who introduced me to digital photography and were a great cheering section, and to my husband Arthur W. Joyce Jr. (Art), who ironed out myriad technical problems and supported me in every other way, as always. My thanks to my editor, Mary Ellen Wilson, who has been a joy to work with and who has shown incredible patience, good judgment, and diligence, and to all the staff in the Publications Department.

Winterthur's Reflecting Pool in May.

Introduction

A Color-Filled Garden

Color, to Henry Francis du Pont, was a "vast field in itself" and, in the garden, "the thing that really counts more than any other." By 1962 du Pont had been gardening for sixty years, and the Garden Club of America had recently named him "perhaps the best gardener this country has ever produced." At his family home, his beloved country estate called Winterthur, he created a garden of surpassing beauty that in its complexity and coherence is a marvel of ingenuity. Plants bloom almost continuously throughout the year, with outstanding areas of color coming into focus in a well-planned sequence. In turn, each area melds seamlessly with its neighbors to form a unified whole. Such sequencing and continuity did not come about without a great deal of work and planning. All told, du Pont devoted some seventy years, a labor of love to be sure, to creating his world-class garden. Today Winterthur's talented horticulturists, with deep respect and devotion, continue to preserve, renew, and amplify his design.

What can we as gardeners, from enthusiastic novices to the more advanced, learn from this beautifully planned landscape and from its creator? Surely many things. In presenting this publication, my colleagues at Winterthur and I offer some of the accumulated wisdom that the garden represents. Winterthur's plants

Spanish bluebells (Hyacinthoides hispanica) *enliven an approach to Azalea Woods.*

are introduced as they appear from month to month, grouped as they are in the garden. This organization brings together plants that bloom at the same time in colors that enhance one another. In addition to groupings, such plants as Virginia bluebells and wild phlox bloom throughout the property and, in their time, "carry the day." These are noteworthy and given their due. Genera such as magnolias, which appear in many places, are, for simplification, addressed together. Azalea Woods, the Sundial Garden, the bog of the Quarry Garden, the fish pools in the Glade Garden, and a patio garden as well as container plants at the Reflecting Pool round out a variety of cultural situations.

We present here practical plants that have stood the test of time, native and non-native, common and unusual. Through his indefatigable searching, H. F. du Pont found countless little-used plants that are both beautiful and easy to grow. Many appear in this guide.

We also illustrate a number of du Pont's design principles. One in particular is soon apparent—there are no fussy mixtures. Scenes are instead painted in what landscape architect William H. Frederick Jr. calls "broad, bold brush strokes" of color—partly because Winterthur is a vast estate and has been invested with plants in proportion to its size but also because this practice was very much a part of du Pont's aesthetic. Photographs presenting "framed views" show us that scenes are often made up of one color and its variations set against a background of greens and neutrals. Such groupings are infinitely peaceful and satisfying. When more than one color is used, we find that the colors are grouped pleasingly but with one color dominating.

Inherent in du Pont's nature were a love of beauty in general, an excellent sense of spatial relations, a penchant for noticing details, and a discriminating awareness of color. He credits much of the development of his talents to growing up among flowers, which if "really seen," he said, would help one appreciate proportion, detail, material, and color. With energy and perseverance, he combined these gifts with a well-organized approach to gardening.

H. F. du Pont had one habit that was particularly instrumental in his success—he was a lifelong, diligent note-taker. He walked in his garden each day when he was in residence, seeing how his "children" were faring, what was in bloom, noticing what might be improved, what needed to be moved, and jotting it all down in a little pocket notebook or in his hardcover diary. When he found a color combination that he liked in his or someone else's garden or at a flower show, he wrote it down. When discovering a new plant, he noted not only the color, which he often related to something he knew (milk white, wax white, etc.), but also other details that were important to him. With daffodils, for instance, he would note the length and strength of the stems and the way the blossoms were held. This businesslike approach to gardening served him well.

Through this largely empirical but organized approach as well as continuous study, du Pont created his magnificent garden. Although few of us have

the vast acres that Winterthur encompasses, we can, as home gardeners, apply du Pont's principles and color combinations on a smaller scale. The Winterthur Garden, as presented in the following pages and as a great living example, provides abundant inspiration.

Using This Book

The Winterthur Garden is arranged as a series of focal areas that take center stage one after another during the year. This guide follows a corresponding pattern. Plants in harmonizing colors that have the same bloom time are grouped here as they are in the garden. These groupings, or garden areas, have descriptive names— such as March Bank, Winterhazel Walk, Azalea Woods, and so on—and can be located on the map on page 15 as well as by signage throughout the garden.

In this guide, a brief description introduces each garden area and places it in the proper seasonal time frame; photographs show plant combinations as well as individual plants. Within the discussion of each area, a section called "In the Home Garden" offers suggestions for possible uses for these combinations or plants in your own garden. "Plant Specifics" includes information about each plant, its cultural requirements, propagation, pruning techniques, and cultivars.

Hardiness zones given for each plant are based on USDA zones and indicate where the plant will usually grow well. A zone in parentheses indicates a marginally safe zone for that plant since viability can vary due to microclimates, soils, and summer conditions, among other factors. See the USDA plant hardiness zone map on page 169.

In the Appendixes, "Gardening Basics" offers practical information about soils, fertilizers, mulches, and record keeping. The "Suggested Reading" section contains an invaluable reference to finding some of the more unusual plants and includes a list of books that many gardeners will want to consult for detailed information on new cultivars, related plants, gardening techniques, and design ideas. Finally, a glossary provides a quick reference to unfamiliar terms you may come across in the text.

Map of the Winterthur Garden and Estate

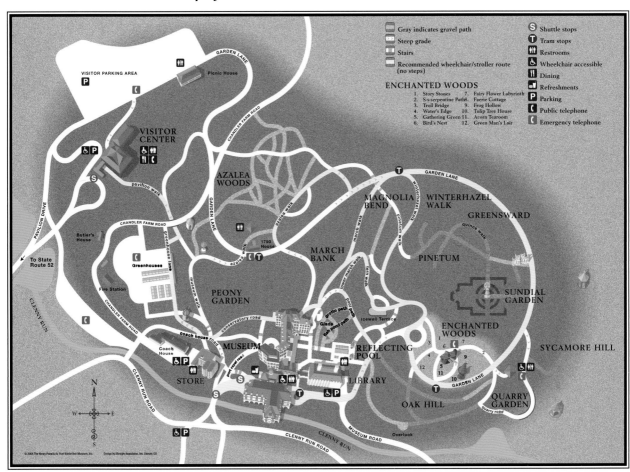

"For years I kept records
of when the first flowers
came out, and I still do
as a matter of fact."

— *H. F. du Pont, 1962*

Winter into Spring

*"There are quite a lot of spring
Snow Drops in the woods."*

—Henry Francis du Pont, January 1934

Finding and reporting on spring's first flowers was a longstanding tradition in the du Pont family. The culmination of this lifelong pleasure is celebrated at Winterthur in three spectacular gardens: March Bank, Winterhazel Walk, and Greensward. These gardens star bulbs, shrubs, and trees that defy cold weather and bring color and life to the waning winter scene. If you are partial to such early arrivals, explore the following pages to discover ways to "turn on" spring in your own garden.

Opener: Suddenly spring — the winter landscape is immediately transformed by the appearance of early-blooming bulbs, such as glory-of-the-snow (Chionodoxa forbesii), massed here on the March Bank. Sheltered by huge deciduous trees, the bank provides an ideal setting for a winter-into-spring panorama.

Left: Bloodroot (Sanguinaria canadensis) *and* Chionodoxa forbesii

MARCH BANK
Late January–April

Winter aconites join snowdrops (Galanthus) *to announce the arrival of spring at Winterthur.*

During January and February, anticipation mounts as the first tentative hints of spring appear in the Winterthur Garden. In March all doubt about this unfolding drama is cast aside. The famous March Bank, with its acres of color and masses of bloom, exuberantly proclaims the arrival of the new growing season. An encore effect ripples throughout the landscape, as drifts and pockets of the same colorful plants—some self-seeded, some purposely sown—delight the winter weary at every turn. Such "bonuses" create a sense of unity and make Winterthur an exceptional early-spring garden. These smaller groupings also suggest ways to bring the colors of the March Bank to our own gardens.

Begun in 1902, March Bank is a superb example

of the theories of nineteenth-century British writer William Robinson. Planted with so-called minor bulbs that increase every year, it has grown into an extensive naturalistic display. The first to flower are snowdrops, diminutive bulbs that create a green-and-white color scheme against the brown of fallen leaves or vestiges of snow. Being weather dependent like other minor bulbs, their exact bloom time will vary. Bright yellow is added to the mix with the appearance of Amur adonis *(Adonis amurensis)* and winter aconites *(Eranthis hyemalis)*, both with round, multipetaled flowers that resemble large buttercups. Adonis tends to be shy and may produce only one significant patch in a garden, but winter aconites are splendid growers that spread famously once established.

Then one day, as if by magic, the bank turns a bright, electric blue. Primarily responsible for this azure phase is glory-of-the-snow *(Chionodoxa forbesii)*, which spills over the edges of the March Bank and has established secondary pools of color at some distance in the landscape. In some areas, Siberian squills *(Scilla siberica)* are planted with it and overlap somewhat in bloom time. Viewed closely, the lavender blue chionodoxa and royal blue scilla do not seem to harmonize; yet interplanted in large numbers,

in the style of H. F. du Pont, they create a smashing effect when they bloom together. In some years, we see instead a neat succession, the scilla emerging as the chionodoxa wanes. Either plant is lovely by itself as well. Both are excellent multipliers and will give years of pleasure as they increase, chionodoxa spreading over wide areas and scilla forming handsome clumps.

"Good with all the bulbs," said H. F. du Pont of this early-flowering dogwood tree, Cornus officinalis.

Sprinkled along the March Bank are several groups of diminutive yellow daffodils (*Narcissus asturiensis* and others), just enough to heighten the sweep of blue by contrast. At the understory level, du Pont chose *Cornus officinalis*, the Japanese cornel dogwood tree, whose misty yellow flowers make a show in the early spring landscape.

Over time, white snowflakes *(Leucojum vernum)* and purple and white Dutch hybrid crocus (*Crocus* hybrids) make their spring appearances, while white bloodroot *(Sanguinaria canadensis)* arrives later. By the end of March, the bank is thick with the leaves of emerging Virginia bluebells, Italian windflowers, and other naturalized plants holding promise of pleasures to come.

Above: Scilla siberica *(background) massed with chionodoxa (foreground), a lively combination.*

Right: Tiny daffodils are in scale with ground-hugging chionodoxa.

In the Home Garden

The March Bank is an easy type of planting for the home gardener to emulate. The concept is simple: a few hardy plants that spread every year, producing carpets of color in early spring. A group of deciduous trees, especially on a slope, would provide the ideal setting for your own version of the bank. However, you might wish to plant just a few minor bulbs near the entrance to your home. Other possible sites include pockets created by roots of trees, the front of a border, under shrubs, or in a rock garden. Chionodoxa may be used as a drift in your lawn. Since the Robinsonian idea is to select plants that spread, you may decide to plant a lot of bulbs in the beginning or just a few, waiting for a more lavish display in years to come.

Adonis amurensis

ADONIS AMURENSIS
Amur Adonis
Ranunculaceae
Japan and Eastern Asia
Herbaceous perennial. Glossy, yellow, buttercup-like blossoms followed by ferny foliage that lasts until June. Needs 6 weeks of temperatures below 40°F to break dormancy. Does not spread rapidly, but a few plants are effective. Size: 9"–12" tall, 12" spread. Soil: well drained, humus rich. Propagation: division of rhizomes after foliage has died. Sun; partial shade south of zone 5. Zones (3) 4–7.

CHIONODOXA FORBESII
(FORMERLY C. LUCILIAE)
Glory-of-the-Snow
Liliaceae
Asia Minor
Bulb. Lavender-blue, upturned flowers with white eye in early spring. Will grow in a lawn if foliage allowed to ripen before mowing. Size: 4"–6" tall, 4" spread. Soil: well drained, humus rich. Propagation: self-seeds readily; also forms bulblets. Sun to partial shade. Zones (3) 4–8.

CORNUS OFFICINALIS
Japanese Cornel Dogwood
Cornaceae
Japan, Korea
Deciduous tree. Airy, yellow blossoms appear before leaves and when few other trees or shrubs are in bloom. Size: 20'–25' tall, 35' spread. Soil: well drained, humus rich. Propagation: softwood cuttings; difficult. Sun to partial shade. Zones 5–8.

Crocus, with *Chionodoxa forbesii*

CROCUS, DUTCH HYBRIDS
Common Garden Crocus
Iridaceae
Parentage variable
Herbaceous plant; grows from corms. Yellow, white, or purple chalice-shape flowers in early spring. Few pests or diseases, but corms occasionally eaten by mice or squirrels. Size: 5" tall, 6" spread. Soil: well drained, humus rich. Propagation: separation of cormels in fall. Sun to light shade. Zones 4–8.

Eranthis hyemalis

ERANTHIS HYEMALIS
Winter Aconite
Ranunculaceae
Western Europe
Herbaceous perennial. Yellow buttercup-like flowers surrounded by green bracts that form a "ruff." Plant tubers in early fall after soaking briefly in water. Size: 4"–6" tall, 4" spread. Soil: fertile, well drained. Propagation: Self-seeding or division of tubers. Sun to partial shade. Zones 3–7.

Galanthus elwesii

GALANTHUS
Snowdrop
Amaryllidaceae
Bulb. Straplike foliage, white flowers in late winter. Soil: well drained, humus rich. Propagation: offsets, seeds. Sun to partial shade. Zones (3) 4–7. Found on the March Bank are *G. elwesii* (giant snowdrop), Asia Minor, size: 9"–12" tall, 6" spread; and *G. nivalis* (common snowdrop), northern Europe, size: 6"–9" tall, 12" spread.

LEUCOJUM VERNUM
Spring Snowflake
Amaryllidaceae

Leucojum vernum

Central Europe
Bulb. White, nodding flowers that look like ballerina skirts, each segment tipped with green. Size: 10"–12" tall, 10" spread. Soil: adaptable, moisture tolerant. Propagation: offsets. Sun to partial shade. Zones 3–9.

Narcissus asturiensis

NARCISSUS ASTURIENSIS
Asturian Daffodil
Amaryllidaceae
Spain and Portugal
Bulb. Yellow, trumpet-type miniature daffodil. Very early blooming. Size: 5"–7" tall,

4" spread. Soil: well drained. Propagation: seeds or offsets. *N. minor, N. minor* var. *minimus, N. nanus*, and others listed in catalogues as early, yellow, and 5"–10" in height would do well in a planting of *Chionodoxa forbesii* and/or *Scilla siberica*. Sun. Zones 4–9.

SANGUINARIA CANADENSIS
Bloodroot
Papaveraceae
Eastern N. America

Herbaceous perennial. Flowers with pure white petals and yellow stamens emerge from a distinctive rolled, lobed leaf. Red sap, rhizomes, and stems. Foliage dies down by late summer. Soil: moist, well drained, neutral

Sanguinaria canadensis

to slightly acid. Size: 3"–6" tall, 8" spread. Propagation: self-sowing or division after flowering. Cultivar: 'Multiplex,' a double form. Partial shade to shade. Zones 3–8 (9).

Scilla siberica

SCILLA SIBERICA
Siberian Squill
Liliaceae
Siberia

Bulb. Royal blue, nodding flowers. Straplike foliage. Size: 3"–6" tall, 4" spread. Soil: well drained. Propagation: self-seeds; separation of offsets. Cultivar/Related Species: 'Spring Beauty' grows at Winterthur, along with *S. bifolia*, two-leaved squill. Sun or partial shade. Zones 2–7.

JOHNNY APPLESEEDING

March Bank horticulturist Carol Long practices what she calls Johnny Appleseeding. In April she watches for the developing seed heads of spring bulbs that she wants to increase and, as they ripen, distributes the seeds in places where she wants them to grow. Later in the year she helps along wildflowers in the same way. This practice is a refinement of William Robinson's theories, for he advocated allowing plants to spread as they would, a method that is also practical.

WINTERHAZEL WALK
Early April–Early May

After the exhilarating bloom of spring bulbs, gardeners look for plants that will continue to bring life and color to the home landscape. Winterthur's Winterhazel Walk offers an intriguing array of shrubs and underplantings with appealing colors and exceptionally early bloom.

Forming the backbone of the walk are two shrubs: pale yellow winterhazel (*Corylopsis* spp. and cv.) and rosy lavender Korean rhododendron *(Rhododendron mucronulatum)*. H. F. du Pont first observed this combination in his garden around 1920, noting that these

Winterhazel and Korean rhododendron in full bloom in earliest spring is decidedly misty and ethereal.

Asian plants bloomed at the same time and that their "chemistry" was just right. He then built an entire walk around them, adding underplantings for variety and enhancement. The colors of both plants also go remarkably well with the lavender blue of *Chionodoxa forbesii*, still in bloom nearby.

ACCOMPANIMENTS

Growing in smaller numbers in the Winterhazel Walk are three harmonizing shrubs, one offering early foliage and two extending the bloom season.

Cherry prinsepia *(Prinsepia sinensis)* has foliage and straw yellow blooms that appear as early as the flowers of corylopsis and Korean rhododendron and mix well with them. A shrub with attractive, arching branches, prinsepia is easy to grow and pest free (although thorn bearing). Continuing the color scheme and extending the bloom season are Keisk rhododendron *(Rhododendron keiskei)*, an exquisite pale yellow shrub, and *R. yedoense* var. *poukhanense*, commonly called Korean azalea (as distinct from Korean rhododendron), in rosy lavender. These shrubs bloom together in late April, after the main flowering of the Winterhazel Walk has passed.

In addition, several low, herbaceous plants in lavender, mauve, chartreuse, and pale yellow bloom

in timely fashion to echo the colors of the shrubs. Hybrids of *Helleborus orientalis*, the Lenten rose, in shades of white to mauve, line a path called the Hellebore Walk. Partway along the walk, *H. foetidus*, or bearsfoot hellebore, introduces a ribbon of chartreuse. Since the "blossoms" of the hellebores are made up of sepals rather than petals, they last a long time and are still showy in May, when false Solomon's seal *(Smilacina racemosa)* blooms with greenish ivory plumes, unifying the color scheme. By this time, *H. foetidus* has put up narrow splays of dark green foliage, ferns have unfurled, and the Hellebore Walk has become a most attractive woodland garden.

Another herbaceous plant with a harmonizing color and appropriate bloom time is bulb corydalis *(Corydalis bulbosa* sbsp. *densiflora)*, whose delicate mauve blossoms end in saucy little upturned spurs. A mass planting of these 8-inch plants is soft and appealing. *Narcissus* 'Hunter's Moon,' an early-blooming pale yellow daffodil, further strengthens the yellow theme.

Other plants that du Pont used from time to time on the Winterhazel Walk are pasque flower *(Anemone pulsatilla)*, with rosy lavender flowers, and two primulas: drumstick primrose *(Primula denticulata)*, with soft lavender globelike flower heads, and abchasica primrose *(P. vulgaris* var. *abchasica)*, with deep rich cerise and gold flowers.

"Good for early green," said du Pont of Prinsepia sinensis.

In the Home Garden

Corylopsis and Korean rhododendron bring many assets to a mixed shrub border. After its early flowering, corylopsis gradually becomes straw yellow, as papery bracts remain when the petals fall. As such, it will brighten a border for weeks in early spring and mix well with later-blooming shrubs.

Gradually bringing forth leaves of golden green, it continues to add a bright note to the border and provides an excellent foil for other colors. Both corylopsis and Korean rhododendron are splendid subjects for indoor forcing of early spring flowers and will develop excellent fall color as well.

Hellebores also provide a bonus, with dark green, glossy foliage that persists through mild winter months. Cut blossoms floated in a bowl last well. Rhododendron yedoense var. poukhanense might be just what you need for a sunny spot, for it is an azalea that thrives in full sun.

Corydalis bulbosa sbsp. *densiflora*

CORYDALIS BULBOSA SBSP. DENSIFLORA
Bulb Corydalis
Fumariaceae
Europe, Asia

Herbaceous perennial; grows from a cormlike tuber. In earliest spring, 10–20 flowers appear on each upright stem. Handsome leaves, much divided. Propagation: seed, sown as soon as ripe. Size: 8" tall, equal spread. Soil: evenly moist, near neutral pH. Partial shade. Zones 5–8. Suitable substitute: *C. solida*.

Corylopsis 'Winterthur'

CORYLOPSIS
Winterhazel
Hamamelidaceae
Four types of corylopsis grow in this area. All are deciduous shrubs with primrose yellow flowers in slender, pendulous clusters in earliest spring, before leaves. Heights, flowering characteristics differ. Like many in the witch-hazel family, corylopsis is pest free, though open flowers may be damaged by late frosts. Propagation: softwood cuttings.

C. pauciflora (buttercup winterhazel), Japan and Taiwan. Dainty, fragrant flowers in clusters of 2–3. Size: 4'–6' tall, 6' wide. Soil: moist, well drained. Partial shade. Zones 6–8. *C. platypetala*, China. Flowers in clusters of 8–20, each about 2" long. Size: 8'–10' tall, 10' spread. Soil: moist, well drained, acid. Sun to partial shade. Zones 6–8. *C. spicata* (spike corylopsis), Japan. Purplish emerging foliage; forms clusters of 6–12. Size: 4'–6' tall, 6' spread. Soil: fertile, acid or neutral. Sun to partial shade. Zones 5–8. *C.* 'Winterthur' (Winterthur corylopsis), fragrant hybrid available commercially, thought to be a cross between *C. spicata* and *C. pauciflora*. Clusters of 4–10 flowers. Size: 6' tall, equal spread. Soil: moist, well drained, acid, humus rich. Sun to partial shade. Zones 6–8.

HELLEBORUS ORIENTALIS
(SYN. H. x HYBRIDUS)
Lenten Rose
Ranunculaceae
Asia Minor
Herbaceous perennial. Saucerlike blossoms in white, mauve, purple, some greenish, some spotted. Broad, palmate leaves. Easy to grow. Size 18" tall, 15" wide. Soil: moist, well drained (although will tolerate heavier, slightly alkaline soil). Propagation: self-sows; division of clumps not advised. Partial shade.

Helleborus orientalis

Zones 4–8 (9). Related species: *H. foetidus* (bearsfoot hellebore), Europe. Chartreuse or light green cup-shape blossoms on ends of branched stems. Narrow, palmate leaves. Size: 18"–24" tall, 18" spread. Zones 5–7 (8).

Narcissus 'Hunter's Moon'

NARCISSUS 'HUNTER'S MOON'
Hunter's Moon Daffodil
Amaryllidaceae

Bulb. Early, pale yellow trumpet daffodil. If hard to find, substitute similar available narcissus. Size: 18"–20" tall, 10" spread. Soil:

well drained, humus rich, neutral to slightly acid. Propagation: offsets. Sun to partial shade. Zones 3–8.

PRINSEPIA SINENSIS
Cherry Prinsepia
Rosaceae
Manchuria

Deciduous shrub. Small, pale yellow flowers, early foliage on arching branches. Pest free. Size: 6'–10' tall, 10' spread. Soil: adaptable. Propagation: seed, softwood cuttings. Sun. Zones 4–7.

Rhododendron yedoense var. *poukhanense*

RHODODENDRON
Azaleas and Rhododendrons
Ericaceae

Three species of rhododendron grow on the Winterhazel Walk. Soil: acid, moist, well drained, organically rich. For detailed information, see "Other Noteworthy Azaleas and Rhododendrons" (page 77).

    R. keiskei (Keisk rhododendron), Japan. Low-growing evergreen shrub; clusters of soft yellow funnel-form flowers in early to mid spring. Size: 4'–5' tall, 5' spread. Partial

shade. Zones 5–8. *R. mucronulatum* (Korean rhododendron), China, Korea, Japan. Deciduous shrub; flowers appear very early, before leaves. Trouble free. Size: 4'–8' tall, 4'–8' spread. Partial shade. Cultivar: 'Cornell Pink.' Zones: 4–7. *R. yedoense* var. *poukhanense* (Korean azalea), Korea. Evergreen shrub; funnel-shape blossoms in clusters of 2–4. Size: 3'–4' tall, 6' spread. Sun or partial shade. Zones (4) 5–7.

Smilacina racemosa

SMILACINA RACEMOSA
False Solomon's Seal
Liliaceae
N. America

Herbaceous perennial, easy to grow. Ivory plumes on arching stems. Alternate broad, pointed leaves. Red berries. Size: 2'–3' tall, 4' spread. Soil: moist, acid, humus rich. Propagation: division in spring or fall. Partial shade to shade. Zones 3–7 (8).

GREENSWARD
Early April

A planting organized around a limited palette (here, shades of pink) can be singularly satisfying.

If you have a penchant for pink, Winterthur's Greensward is worth investigating. Located in an open allée near the Winterhazel Walk, this collection includes several shrubs and exceptionally beautiful cherry trees.

Among the trees that provide height and significance to the group is the exquisite cherry called Accolade (*Prunus* 'Accolade'). A nice size for the home garden, it is covered with soft, semidouble, white blossoms tinged with pink, which combine well with nearby shrubs that flower in shades of pink and white. Such shrubs include fragrant viburnums *(V. farreri)*, pink and white Nanking cherries *(Prunus tomentosa)*, and vibrant pink Cornell Pink rhododendron *(R. mucronulatum* 'Cornell Pink')*. These plants flower at overlapping times, adding interest for several weeks.

Just across Garden Lane, two huge Sargent cherries *(Prunus sargentii)*, with pink-tinged white blossoms, counterbalance this group. If you have a generous space, you may want to grow one or more of these magnificent trees.

In timely fashion, rare rhododendrons at the edge of Azalea Woods put forth lovely pink trusses that remain effective for several weeks. Farges rhododendron *(R. oreodoxa* var. *fargesii)* produces an unparalleled bloom spectacle in earliest spring. Gardeners who like a challenge, or those in more southerly climes, may want to try this rhododendron for early flowering.

White blossoms of Prunus sargentii *gradually take on a pinkish cast, harmonizing with pink and white plants of the Greensward as well as rosy lavender Korean rhododendron (foreground).*

Prunus tomentosa *and Cornell Pink rhododendron bloom under a young Accolade cherry tree.*

In the Home Garden

Although some cherries may be short-lived and somewhat trouble prone, both Accolade and Sargent cherries have proved themselves dependable. Grouped with Cornell Pink rhododendron and some of the feathery pink or white shrubs described here, either cherry would make a delightful corner or island planting for a home property.

Prunus 'Accolade'

PRUNUS
Rosaceae

The genus *Prunus* includes cherries, peaches, apricots, plums, and almonds. The two cherry trees and one shrub included here are deciduous and have flowers that appear before the leaves. Propagation: softwood cuttings. Soil: adaptable.

　　P. **'Accolade'** (Accolade cherry), parents from Japan (hybrid of *P. sargentii* x *P. subhirtella*). Tree with semidouble, pink-blushed white blossoms and deeper pink buds that hang from long pedicels in early spring. Size: 20'–25' tall, 25' spread. Sun to partial shade. Zones 4–7(8). *P.* **sargentii** (Sargent cherry), Japan. Handsome, huge spreading tree; clusters of single white flowers become pink. Excellent fall color. Size: 20'–50' tall, equal spread. Sun. Zones 4–7. *P.* **tomentosa** (Nanking cherry), China, Japan. Fragrant, spreading shrub covered with small, single, white or pink flowers in early spring; red fruit. Size: 6'–10' tall, 8'–15' spread. Sun to partial shade. Zones (2) 3–7.

R. oreodoxa var. *fargesii*

RHODODENDRON
Rhododendron
Ericaceae
Parentage varies

Two early-blooming rhododendrons are described below. Soil: acid, moist, well drained, organically rich. For detailed information, see "Other Noteworthy Azaleas and Rhododendrons" (page 77). *R.* **oreodoxa var. fargesii** (Farges rhododendron), China. Evergreen, large-leaf rhododendron; trusses of 7–10 pink, bell-shape blossoms. Occasionally suffers blossom damage from late frost; may need winter protection, though buds are quite hardy. Size: 6' tall, equal spread. Partial shade. Zones 6–9. **R. mucronulatum 'Cornell Pink'** (Cornell Pink rhododendron), species from China, Korea, Japan. Deciduous shrub; selected cultivar of the species. Vibrant pink blossoms on bare branches in earliest spring. Size: 4'–8' tall, equal spread. Partial shade. Zones 4–7.

VIBURNUM FARRERI
Fragrant Viburnum
Caprifoliaceae
China
Deciduous, upright shrub; trouble free. Deep pink buds; pink flowers in small clusters before the leaves. Lovely scent. Prune after flowering. Size: 8'–12' tall, equal spread. Soil: moist, well drained, slightly acid. Propagation: softwood cuttings. Cultivar: *V. farreri* 'Candidissima' (Candidissima viburnum), white flowers. Sun to partial shade. Zones (4) 5–8.

Viburnum farreri

Rhododendron mucronulatum 'Cornell Pink'

A VALUABLE COLLABORATION

Charles Sprague Sargent, the first director of the Arnold Arboretum in Massachusetts, was a personal friend of H. F. du Pont and his father. The du Ponts supported the arboretum, which in turn sent many newly discovered plants to Winterthur. The Sargent cherries, named for C. S. Sargent, were sent in 1918. At this time, Sargent suggested the creation of the Pinetum, which stands as a fine backdrop for the Greensward and nearby areas.

"We have had a wonderful

spring here. All the

blooming shrubs have

been marvelous and

I enjoyed to the fullest

all the flowers."

— H. F. du Pont, 1942

*S*pring

"*Solomon in all his glory was not arrayed like one of these.*"

—*Matthew 7:29*

In spring all creation seems to burgeon with bloom, affording us a wealth of plants to cultivate and enjoy. In choosing from this cornucopia, you are invited to share in concepts the Winterthur Garden illustrates. Some of its most famous areas — Quince Walk, Sundial Garden, Azalea Woods — are alive with floral combinations at this season that will offer proven delights for your own garden.

Opener: In April, white spirea, pink crabapples, pink flowering almonds, and lilacs play major parts in the Sundial Garden's symphony of color.

Left: Mertensia virginica

FORSYTHIA AND DAFFODILS
Early–Mid April

Forsythia and daffodils are natural companions: both are early-blooming, cheerful plants primarily in shades of yellow. At Winterthur they often mingle in our field of vision as mass plantings seen from a distance. They are easy to grow and long lasting, so du Pont's theories and practices in using them are of special interest.

FORSYTHIA

For plantings throughout the Winterthur Garden, du Pont chose four types of forsythia that offer varying, subtle hues and successive bloom. The first to appear is early forsythia *(Forsythia ovata)*, flowering about two weeks ahead of others and thus of particular appeal for many gardeners. The fountainlike weeping forsythia *(F. suspensa)* harmonizes well with beds of yellow Emperor daffodils *(Narcissus* 'Emperor'). Noteworthy for its prolific bloom is border forsythia *(F. x intermedia)*; its parent, greenstem forsythia *(F. viridissima)*, blooms a little later. Both arch gracefully. Since forsythia blooms when it is leafless, its yellows show up well against dark evergreens such as pines or other conifers.

Weeping forsythia (Forsythia suspensa) *blooms with Emperor daffodils at Winterthur's Magnolia Bend.*

Mutually enhancing Forsythia viridissima *and brown stone.*

DAFFODILS

Du Pont's affection for daffodils (*Narcissus* species and cultivars) is apparent in April, when great drifts begin blooming on meadows and hillsides, in valleys and woodlands, and along the stream Clenny Run. From long observation, du Pont developed definite ideas about how best to use daffodils; he considered "hit-or-miss" mixtures a "perfect nightmare" and preferred planting cultivars in groups, aiming for a "bold expanse" of each variety. He also felt that daffodils blooming at different times should be kept separate so that fading blooms would not detract from opening ones.

Du Pont further advocated the separation of daffodils with blue-white petals from those with cream-white ones. Along Clenny Run, he used only the cream-white, small-cupped daffodil 'Queen of the North' to create one of his most effective plantations.

PINK DAFFODILS AND A MAPLE

When daffodils with a pink-tinged trumpet became available after 1939, du Pont chose 'Mrs. R. O. Backhouse' *(right)* to plant under his cut-leaf Japanese maple (*Acer palmatum* var. *dissectum*) at Magnolia Bend *(below)*. Such pink- to apricot-colored daffodils, readily available today, make congenial companions to plants with rust-colored foliage.

A sweeping planting of daffodils seems to direct the course of Clenny Run.

PLANT SPECIFICS

In the Home Garden

For our own gardens, forsythias and daffodils may be pleasantly interspersed along a shrub border, set against a backdrop of pines, or simply allowed to bloom together in different parts of the landscape. Daffodils are unusually long-lived, and bulbs are rodent proof, as are other members of the Amaryllis family, so thoughtful selection and placement will give pleasure for years to come.

ACER PALMATUM VAR. DISSECTUM
Cut-Leaf Japanese Maple
Aceraceae
Japan, China, Korea
Small tree or shrub. Reddish foliage, finely cut leaves. Slow growing. Size: 6'–12' tall, equal spread (cultivars may vary). Many cultivars available. Soil: moist, well drained, acidic. Propagation: difficult. Sun to dappled shade. Zones (5) 6–8.

Forsythia viridissima

FORSYTHIA
Forsythia
Oleaceae
Deciduous shrub. Early yellow bloom, before leaves. Fast growing, pest free, durable. Prune after flowering by cutting old branches near plant base. Propagation: softwood or hardwood cuttings. Many cultivars. Soil: adaptable. Sun.

    F. **x** *intermedia* (border forsythia), hybrid, parents from Asia. Size: 8'–10' tall, 10'–12' spread. Zones 6–8. *F. ovata* (early forsythia), Korea. Flower-bud hardy. Size: 4'–6' tall, equal spread. Zones 4–7. *F. suspensa* (weeping forsythia), China. Size: 8'–10' tall,

Forsythia ovata

10'–15' spread. Zones 5–8. *F. viridissima* (greenstem forsythia), China. Size: 6–10' tall, equal spread. Zones 5–8.

NARCISSUS
SPECIES AND CULTIVARS
Daffodils
Amaryllidaceae
Originally Europe, N. Africa
Fall-planted bulbs increase for years. Yellow, cream, white, apricot, or bicolored blossoms of various shapes in early spring. Upright stems, bladelike foliage. A wide variety of daffodils flourish at Winterthur, some no longer available commercially. Numerous hybrids, cultivars, species listed

Narcissus 'Sir Francissus Drake,'
an heirloom daffodil.

in current catalogues will fill most present-
day needs. Soil: well drained, neutral to
slightly acid. Sun or partial shade (partial
shade will produce a deeper color in pink
or apricot daffodils).

Narcissus 'Queen of the North'

N. 'Emperor,' large-cupped, yellow
flowers. Size: 16"–18" tall, 12" spread.
Suitable substitute: *N.* 'Carlton.' Zones 3–7.
N. 'Mrs. R. O. Backhouse,' delicate apricot
cup and white petals on strong stems. Size:
16"–18" tall, 12" spread. Zones 3–7. **N.
'Queen of the North,'** small-cupped daffodil,
white with yellow cup. Size: 12"–15" tall, 12"
spread. Zones 3–7.

HILLS OF DAFFODILS

Most daffodils require good drainage; planting on slopes is ideal.
To attain natural-looking daffodil beds on hillsides, du Pont used
an ingenious method of forming outlines with fallen branches
(stripped of their side shoots) to create pleasing, free-form shapes.
He planted bulbs within these irregular outlines, adding one
or two to fill in where needed. This technique can also be used
to create island beds around a group of trees or to arrange
perennials in borders.

WILDFLOWERS OF SPRING
April–May

Grouped here are both native and non-native plants whose ability to spread by self-seeding or other means gives them the charm and informality characteristic of wildflowers. Each, in its season, adds much delight to garden walks, and any would make a valuable addition to the home garden. Some such plants you will find listed with specific garden areas; others, more widespread, are described here.

Italian windflower (Anemone apennina) *thrives particularly in Azalea Woods and on the March Bank.*

ITALIAN WINDFLOWER

In early April on the March Bank, in Azalea Woods, and in other woodland shelters, we find great floral carpets of the jaunty, upturned faces of Italian windflowers *(Anemone apennina)*. These little daisylike flowers, mostly white or lavender (with the harmonious variations found in colonies of seedlings), have yellow centers and foliage that is deeply cut and attractive. The blossoms close in rainy weather but on sunny days produce a scene as remarkable for its simplicity as for its effectiveness.

SPRING STARFLOWER

Also in early April a mass of palest blue, starlike blossoms, no more than six inches high, appears just below the stone wall of the Pinetum. Spring starflower *(Ipheion uniflorum)*, a little-known bulb, blooms here in the grass,

Beginning in mid April at Winterthur, woods, valleys, and pathways are saturated with the distinctive hue of Virginia bluebells.

where its color blends with crabapples, quince, and viburnums. Having escaped cultivation, this plant has become naturalized in some parts of the country; it will even grow in a pot as a houseplant. Fragrance and delicate color make it especially appealing. Plants become dormant and disappear in late spring, but new foliage emerges in fall and lasts through winter (and should not be mown).

VIRGINIA BLUEBELLS

Certain plants appear in such great numbers and are so widespread that when in bloom, their radiance permeates the entire Winterthur landscape. Among these are Virginia bluebells *(Mertensia virginica)*, or Brandywine bluebells, as they are sometimes called. Blooming in clusters of hanging "bells," this plant is native to the eastern United States and would be ideal for a partially shaded spot in the home garden. The buds are pink but open into a blue flower—one of nature's surprises. If content, these plants will colonize an area without becoming invasive. Their foliage, which arrives early, disappears by summertime, thus giving neighboring perennials elbowroom or providing space for annuals. In warmer climates, they appreciate a moist situation.

SOLOMON'S SEAL AND FALSE SOLOMON'S SEAL

Solomon's seal *(Polygonatum biflorum)* and false Solomon's seal *(Smilacina racemosa)* are native plants that thrive in moist, shady situations. They have similar foliage and look somewhat alike before they flower. In bloom, however, they are easily differentiated. "True" Solomon's seal has small, pendulous flowers arranged in pairs at

Spring starflower (Ipheion uniflorum) *adds ground-level interest to nearby crabapples, quince, and viburnums.*

the leaf axils, whereas false Solomon's seal has a generous plume at the end of the stem and is quite a bit showier. Both types of inflorescence are greenish white and appear during May.

DAME'S ROCKET

Among plants that have proved effective and practical at Winterthur, yet are not well known, is *Hesperis matronalis*, or dame's rocket. This appealing plant looks much like the tall phlox of summer gardens *(Phlox paniculata)* but is different in several ways. Dame's rocket has four petals rather than five, and it grows in the shade and blooms in May, whereas garden phlox thrives in midsummer sun. After long naturalization at Winterthur, the colors of dame's rocket are mixed, ranging from white through mauve and purple. When cultivated in gardens, however, the colors are often grown separately. The white form is especially effective in shady spots, and double forms are now available. Technically a biennial, dame's rocket self-sows readily, and established plants sometimes persist for years. Also called sweet rocket, its fragrance is particularly noticeable in the evening. Butterflies find it attractive.

WILD BLUE PHLOX

Wild blue phlox *(Phlox divaricata)* is true to its botanical name: *divaricata* means "spreading," and spread it does!

Yet its soft lavender color is so pleasing in great drifts that most gardeners will not mind this tendency. This phlox is low growing (about a foot high), undemanding, and if taking up too much room, easy to pull up. It likes shade but will tolerate a fair amount of sun. In early May at Winterthur, its pale lavender blooms color the paths, highways and byways, woods and dells, creating delightful vistas.

Phlox divaricata *spreads to form drifts of soft lavender.*

PLANT SPECIFICS

In the Home Garden

*Any or all of these plants will con-
tribute handsomely to shady or partly
shady spots in a home garden, adding
refreshing color to a perennial bed or
under shrubs in a border. The low growers, such as anemone and ipheion,
would prosper in a rockery or along a
path. Solomon's seal and false
Solomon's seal are well suited to a
woodland setting. All are easy to grow
and will add a naturalistic touch to
your spring garden.*

White *Hesperis matronalis*, with hosta foliage

Anemone apennina

ANEMONE APENNINA
Italian Windflower
Ranunculaceae
S. Europe
Low herbaceous plants. White to lavender
daisylike blossoms. Handsome, deeply
cut leaves die down in early summer. Size:
about 9" tall, equal spread. Soil: woodsy,
high organic content. Dappled shade.
Propagation: self-seeds or divide in early
summer. Zones 5–7.

HESPERIS MATRONALIS
Dame's Rocket
Brassicaceae
Europe, Asia
Herbaceous biennial; easy to grow. White,
mauve, or purple phloxlike flowers on tall
stems. Evening fragrance. Cultivars: 'Alba,'
good white; 'Alba-plena,' double white.
Size: 2'–3' tall, 3' spread. Soil: well drained,
adaptable. Sun to dappled shade. Propagation: self-seeds. Zones 3–8 (9).

Ipheion uniflorum

IPHEION UNIFLORUM
Spring Starflower
Alliaceae
Argentina, Uruguay
Bulb. Pale blue or lavender starlike flowers
in April; long-lasting bloom. Straplike foliage
reappears in fall, lasts through winter. Easy,

trouble-free plants that spread and naturalize or can be divided after flowering. Cultivars available. Size: 4"–6" tall, 8" spread. Soil: well drained. Sun to partial shade. Zones 5–9.

Mertensia virginica

MERTENSIA VIRGINICA
Virginia Bluebells
Boraginaceae
Eastern U.S.

Easy-to-grow wildflower. Oval leaves appear early, followed by pink buds that turn to nodding, blue flowers. Dies down in summer. Propagation: self-sows; also division of tubers in fall. Size: 1'–2' tall, equal spread. Soil: moist, well drained. Partial shade. Zones 3–8.

Phlox divaricata

PHLOX DIVARICATA
Wild Blue Phlox
Polemoniaceae
Eastern N. America

Herbaceous perennial. Dark green leaves; flat, lavender blue, 5-petaled flowers.
Cultivars: 'Laphamii,' deeper blue; 'Fuller's White,' an excellent white; many others. Propagation: self-sows, spreads by rhizomes, and roots at nodes. Size: 12"–15" tall, 12" spread. Soil: moist, well drained. Partial shade to sun. Zones 3–8 (9).

Polygonatum biflorum

POLYGONATUM BIFLORUM
Solomon's Seal

Liliaceae
Eastern N. America

Herbaceous perennial. Large, oval leaves alternate along an arching stem. Pairs of greenish white, bell-shape flowers hang at leaf nodes. Look for the "seal" on the rhizomes. Propagation: division in fall. Size: 1'–3' tall, 1'–2' spread. Soil: moist. Partial shade to shade. Zones 3–8 (9).

Smilacina racemosa

SMILACINA RACEMOSA
False Solomon's Seal
Liliaceae
N. America

Easy-to-grow herbaceous perennial. Greenish white plumes on arching stems. Alternating broad, pointed leaves. Berries turn red. Propagation: division in spring or fall. Size: 2–3' tall, 4' spread. Soil: moist, acid, humus rich. Partial shade to shade. Zones 3–7 (8).

Rhododendron *'Conewago' blooms beside a venerable collection of saucer magnolias at Winterthur's Magnolia Bend.*

MAGNOLIA BEND
April–June

Magnolias are decidedly elegant, distinguished and pleasing in all aspects—leaves, branching patterns, flowers, and fruits. Despite their singular elegance, however, magnolias are quite easy to grow.

In April Magnolia Bend is abloom with venerable saucer magnolias *(Magnolia* x *soulangiana)*, now more than one hundred years old. Their lovely wine, pink, and ivory chalices characteristically show deeper shades at the base, lighter shades above, and a velvety ivory lining. Favorite cultivars at Winterthur, all famous, are the pinkish Rustica Rubra and San Jose, rosy Alexandrina, and deep rose-purple Lennei. Their colors combine beautifully with the pinkish lavender, ball-like trusses of Conewago rhododendron (*R.* 'Conewago').

Saucer magnolias bloom in the Sundial Garden as well, forming a backdrop for the lower-growing plants. Here also is the rare magnolia Wada's Memory, appearing as a great white egg-shape tree. In several places in the landscape, star magnolias (*M. stellata*) bear white straplike blossoms, while the white blossoms of yulan

White, strawberry-throated blossoms of
Rhododendron mucronatum *'Magnifica,'*
lavender camassia, and purple Siberian iris bloom
together in May.

magnolias *(M. denudata)* emerge chalice shaped and gradually open. Late frosts may damage blossoms on these spring-blooming magnolias but will not harm the trees themselves where they are otherwise hardy.

June is the month when two native magnolias begin to flower, both with a refreshing lemon scent. Sweetbay magnolia *(M. virginiana)* is a graceful tree with delicate, white blossoms and silver-lined leaves, while the magnificent southern magnolia *(M. grandiflora)*, over a period of several weeks, unfurls ivory petals of great size and substance to form bowl-shape blossoms with pale yellow centers.

MAGNOLIA BEND IN MAY AND JUNE

Other plants bring color to Magnolia Bend later in the year. In May the area is a delight of whites and soft pastels. The foundation is a planting of *Rhododendron mucronatum* 'Magnifica,' which bears large, white blossoms with strawberry-speckled throats, producing an effect of palest pink. Close by, feathery spires of camassia *(Camassia cusickii)* bloom in delicate lavender blue, while rich purple Siberian iris *(Iris siberica* 'Perry's Blue') adds punch here and there. Stone steps lead to a lower level of Magnolia Bend, where some lesser-known lilacs *(Syringa* species and a hybrid) accompany a planting of azaleas *(Rhododendron* cultivars) in pinks, lavender, and mauve.

In the nearby woodlands grow doublefile viburnums *(V. plicatum* var. *tomentosum)*, plants as charming as they are dependable. Set in the deep green woods, they are lovely in May, with their gracefully arching branches bearing white, lacy blossoms. They will also grow in sunny spots, becoming a fuller plant with more horizontal branching. A new cultivar called Summer Snowflake grows at Magnolia Bend; during the summer, it has repeat blooming that is less profuse but no less attractive.

Variations on a theme: lilacs and azaleas in pink, lavender, and mauve at Winterthur's Magnolia Bend.

In June three white roses bloom at Magnolia Bend. They are *Rosa rugosa* hybrids chosen for their good-looking foliage, ease of care, and beautiful blossoms. *Rosa* 'Henry Hudson' has double white flowers that contrast nicely with its deep pink buds and richly colored green foliage. *R.* 'Schneckoppe' is also a double white but shows a bit of pink when open. *R.* 'Blanc Double de Coubert,' an old favorite, is a pure white double to semidouble that is fragrant, vigorous, and hardy. All feature the quilted leaves that *rugosa* (meaning "wrinkled") suggests. Bloom continues sporadically during the summer and increases again in the fall, when orange-red hips (fruits) add interest.

White rugosa roses, here R. 'Blanc Double de Coubert,' blend seamlessly with nearby magnolias.

PLANT SPECIFICS

In the Home Garden

Magnolia x soulangiana is a favorite magnolia for home landscaping. It is adaptable to many climates, produces handsome colors in early spring, and is moderately sized, growing as either a multistemmed shrub or a tree. Ease of culture and blooming when young add to its popularity. M. stellata *and* M. denudata *are other early bloomers that are a convenient size for home grounds. Modestly sized* M. virginiana *blooms later and can tolerate, but does not require, fairly damp soils.* M. grandiflora, *where hardy, is large and magnificent. Of the later-blooming plants growing here, doublefile viburnum is a treasure in sun or shade. The lilacs, although they are lesser-known types, should be more widely used—they are prolific bloomers, adaptable, disease resistant, and of modest size. Rugosa roses are quite trouble free and adaptable. They will grow at the shore and in cold climates.*

CAMASSIA CUSICKII
Cusick Camas
Liliaceae
Oregon
Bulb. Racemes of pale lavender-blue flowers arise from a basal cluster of bladelike leaves. Propagation: offsets. Size: 2'–3' tall, 2' spread. Soil: moist in spring. Sun to partial shade. Zones (3) 4–8.

IRIS SIBERICA 'PERRY'S BLUE'
Perry's Blue Siberian Iris
Iridaceae
Species: Central Europe, Russia
Herbaceous perennial. Erect, fleur-de-lis-type flowers of rich purple. Bladelike foliage. Likes moist situation. Clumps expand; divide only as necessary. Innumerable other cultivars. Size: 2'–3' tall, 2' spread. Soil: moist, good garden. Sun to partial shade. Zones 3–9.

MAGNOLIA
Magnolia
Magnoliaceae
Blossoms of early-blooming types sometimes damaged by frost. Propagation: cuttings of firm wood. Prune as necessary, even larger branches. Soil: moist, well drained, acid; *M. virginiana* will tolerate wet soil.

M. DENUDATA (HEPTAPETA)
Yulan Magnolia
China
Deciduous tree. White, chalicelike blossoms, gradually spreading open, appear before

Magnolia denudata

handsome, roundish foliage. Trouble free, adaptable. Size: 30'–40' tall, 25'–30' spread. Sun or partial shade. Zones 5–8.

Magnolia grandiflora evergreen foliage

M. GRANDIFLORA
Southern Magnolia
Southeastern U.S.
One of the region's most beautiful trees. Evergreen, glossy, leathery leaves often backed with brown indumentum (felt). Ivory, bowl-shape flowers in summer; lemonlike fragrance. Sometimes espaliered and kept smaller. In colder climates, avoid winter sun and wind through careful siting. Many culti-

vars, some with improved hardiness, smaller size. Size: 60'–80' tall, 30'–50' spread. Sun or partial shade. Zones (6) 7–9 (10).

Magnolia x *soulangiana* 'Rustica Rubra'

M. x SOULANGIANA
Saucer Magnolia
Parents: China

Small tree or shrub. Chalice-shape blossoms in wine, pink, and white appear in early spring, before leaves. Flowering begins at an early age. Many cultivars. Size: 20'–30' tall, equal spread. Soil: moist, well drained, acid. Sun. Zones 4–9.

M. STELLATA
Star Magnolia
Japan

Deciduous tree or shrub. Blossoms are white with many straplike tepals (petals); fragrant. Blooms early, before the leaves. Many cultivars, some pink. Adaptable. Size: 15'–20' tall, 10'–15' spread. Sun. Zones 4–8 (9).

M. VIRGINIANA
Sweetbay Magnolia
Eastern U.S.

Tree or shrub; deciduous in the north, semi-

Magnolia *stellata*

evergreen to evergreen in the south. White, fragrant, cup-shape blossoms appear sporadically for several weeks in early summer. Attractive, light green foliage with silver lining. Easy, adaptable. Many cultivars. Size: 10'–20' tall (to 60' in the south), equal spread. Soil: acid, will tolerate wet. Sun or shade. Zones 5–9.

M. 'WADA'S MEMORY'
Wada's Memory Magnolia
Parents: Japan

Large, egg-shape tree covered with white blossoms in April, before the foliage. Size: 30'–40' tall, 20'–30' spread. Sun. Zones 4–8.

Magnolia 'Wada's Memory'

RHODODENDRON
Rhododendron
Ericaceae

Three evergreen azaleas and one semi-evergreen rhododendron grow in this area. Soil: moist, well drained, acid, high organic. For detailed information, see "Other Noteworthy Azaleas and Rhododendrons" (page 77).

R. mucronatum **'Magnifica'** (Magnifica azalea), large, white flowers with strawberry-speckled throat in midspring. Size: 6' tall, 6'–8' spread. Zones 6–9. *R.* **'Lavender Queen'** (Lavender Queen Kurume azalea), parents from Asia. Pinkish lavender flowers in midspring. Size: 4' tall, equal spread. *R.* **'Mauve Beauty'** (Mauve Beauty Kurume

Rhododendron 'Conewago'

azalea), parents from Asia. Mauve flowers in midspring. Size: 4' tall, equal spread. Zones 6–8 (9). **R. 'Conewago'** (*R. carolinianum* x *mucronulatum*, Conewago rhododendron), parents from North Carolina and Japan. Semi-evergreen shrub with pinkish lavender, ball-shape trusses early in spring. Size: 4'–6' tall, 3'–5' spread. Sun to partial shade. Zones (4) 5–8.

ROSA RUGOSA
HYBRIDS
Rugosa Rose Hybrids
Rosaceae
Species: Asia
Rugosas are some of the most trouble-free roses. Fragrant flowers in June; red fruit

Rosa 'Henry Hudson'

beginning in August. Handsome, heavy, quilted foliage; good fall color. Prune in early spring. Propagation: softwood cuttings. Soil: well drained, with organic content, pH adaptable. Sun. Zones 2–7 (8).

'Blanc Double de Coubert,' white double to semidouble; fragrant, vigorous, and hardy. Size: 4'–6' tall, 4' spread. **'Henry Hudson,'** white, double blossoms, pink buds. Size: 3' tall, equal spread. **'Schneckoppe,'** double blossoms, white tinged with pink. Size: 3' tall, equal spread.

SYRINGA
Lilac
Oleaceae
These deciduous lilacs bloom at the same time as *Syringa vulgaris* and cultivars but are more modestly sized and offer variations in textures and habits. Delicately fragrant. Prune after flowering by cutting old canes close to ground. Propagation: softwood cuttings. Soil: neutral, pH adaptable, well drained.

S. laciniata (cutleaf lilac), China. Bushy shrub; deeply lobed leaves, lavender flowers. Feathery texture. Fragrant. Tolerates heat, mildew resistant. Size: 6'–8' tall, 9' spread. Sun; will bloom in some shade. Zones 4–8. *S. meyeri* (Meyer lilac), China. Rounded shrub; lavender flowers. Excellent bloomer. Mildew resistant. Size: 4'–8' tall, 6'–12' spread. Sun. Zones 3–7. *S. x persica* (Persian lilac), parents from Iran and Asia. Arching branches, pale lavender flowers borne in profusion. Size: 4'–8' tall, 5'–10' spread. Sun. Zones 3–7.

Viburnum 'Summer Snowflake'

VIBURNUM PLICATUM
VAR. TOMENTOSUM
Doublefile Viburnum
Caprifoliaceae
China, Japan
Deciduous shrub. White, lace-cap flowers in pairs along arching or horizontal branches. Highly decorative. Fairly deep green foliage. Trouble free. Prune after flowering. Propagation: softwood cuttings. Size: 8'–10' tall, 9'–12' spread. Soil: moist, well drained, slightly acid. Sun to partial shade. Zones 5–7 (8). Many cultivars, including **'Summer Snowflake,'** which repeats bloom sporadically throughout summer. Size: 6'–8' tall, equal spread.

QUINCE WALK
April

Flowering quince in full bloom is delightful for borders. It offers an immense color range, from pink and coral to lacquer red.

Under the shelter of great evergreens of the Pinetum, du Pont planted a large collection of quince that now forms the Quince Walk. Pathways are lined with various cultivars that flower in warm tones and create a medley of color.

Flowering quince (*Chaenomeles* species, hybrids, and cultivars) produces blooms in early spring on plants that display a distinctive branching pattern. The little

cup-shape blossoms open in wonderful colors that range from white through pinks and corals to oranges and reds, each blossom centered with bright yellow stamens. Featured prominently in the Quince Walk is the pink-and-white Appleblossom quince (*C. speciosa* 'Appleblossom'), among many others, including the almost lacquer red Rowallane (*C.* x *superba* 'Rowallane'). At the entrance to the walk, du Pont planted two

Chinese snowball viburnums *(Viburnum macrocephalum)* —
a masterstroke since the plants' huge, apple green
budded heads appear just at quince-blossom time,
making the quince colors sing. Later, when the
blossoms are fully open and white, the viburnums
stand like beacons guiding us into the deep green
of the Pinetum.

Also enhancing the quince planting is garland
spirea *(Spiraea* x *arguta)*, which forms delicate, gracefully arching white sprays. These line a path to the
white Latimeria Gates, where a pearl bush *(Exochorda
giraldii* var. *wilsonii)* blooms. Its arching branches
end in long clusters of pure white, ruffled blossoms,
a bit like single roses laced together. The buds
resemble strings of pearls and add immeasurably
to the great appeal of this bush.

*Above: Quince and garland spirea bloom
against a backdrop of evergreens.*

Below: Apple green buds of Viburnum
macrocephalum *enhance the quince colors.*

In the Home Garden

This area presents an adaptable group of plants, including shrubs that bloom in luscious colors, white frothiness, or roselike blossoms. All are happy in either sun or partial shade and are attractive not just in the garden but for arrangements as well.

A smaller version of the pearl bush, Exochorda x macrantha *'The Bride,' is a handsome, sprawling shrub, useful for the home garden.*

If you have room for larger plants, Viburnum macrocephalum, *with its apple green flower heads that later turn white, makes a stunning addition.*

CHAENOMELES SPECIES, HYBRIDS, AND CULTIVARS
Flowering Quince
Rosaceae

Deciduous shrubs. Bloom in early spring, with leaves. Yellow-green fruits appear later. Hybridize freely; innumerable hybrids and cultivars available. Prune after flowering. Propagation: softwood and hardwood cuttings. Soil: well drained, slightly acid. Sun to partial shade.

Most quince species and hybrids have colors that blend well with others. These include **C. japonica** (Japan), orange-red to red blossoms. Size: 3' tall, 3' spread. Zones 4–8. **C. speciosa** (China), red, orange, white,

Heirloom quince, unknown cultivar

or pink blossoms. Size: 6'–10' tall, equal spread. Zones 4–8 (9). **C. x superba** (*C. japonica* x *C. speciosa*), white, pink, orange, or red blossoms. Size: 4'–5' tall, equal spread. Zones 5–8.

Exochorda giraldii var *wilsonii*

EXOCHORDA
Pearl Bush
Rosaceae

Two exochordas are grouped here. Deciduous. White, roselike blossoms in linear clusters, pearl-like buds. Trouble free, durable. Prune after flowering. Propagation: softwood cuttings.

Chaenomeles 'Appleblossom'

Soil: tolerates a wide pH range but likes acid, well drained. Sun to partial shade.

    E. giraldii **var. *wilsonii*** (pearl bush), China. Tall, vase-shape shrub with arching branches. Size: 10'–15' tall, equal spread. Zones (5) 6–7 (8). *E.* **x *macrantha*** 'The Bride' (The Bride pearl bush), parents from Turkistan and China. Low, sprawling shrub, exquisite in its profuse bloom. Size: 3'–4' tall, 4'–6' spread. Zones 5–8.

Spiraea x *arguta*

SPIRAEA x ARGUTA
Garland Spirea
Rosaceae
Parents: Europe and Asia

Deciduous shrub. Arching branches covered with delicate white blossoms in early spring, before leaves. Adaptable, trouble free. Similar to *S. thunbergii*. Prune after flowering by cutting largest canes near ground. Propagation: softwood and hardwood cuttings. Size: 3'–6' tall, equal spread. Soil: any good garden. Sun to partial shade. Zones 4–8.

VIBURNUM MACROCEPHALUM
Chinese Snowball Viburnum
Caprifoliaceae
China

Large-scale shrub, deciduous to semi-evergreen, spectacular in bloom. Apple green buds become white, 3"–8" "snowballs"

about a month later. Prune after flowering. Propagation: cuttings in early summer. Size: 10'–20' tall, equal spread. Soil: moist, well drained, slightly acid. Sun to partial shade. Zones 6–9.

A PERFECT PAIR

The white Latimeria Gates, shown here, were among several garden structures that H. F. du Pont purchased from the Latimer estate in Wilmington, Delaware, in the 1920s. Landscape architect Marian Coffin placed them for him in the garden. In 1929 he wrote to her, "The Exochordas are safely planted." Thus the gates and pearl bushes (*Exochorda giraldii* var. *wilsonii*) have been longtime companions and are as perfectly suited today as when they were first paired more than seventy years ago.

SUNDIAL GARDEN
April–Early May

The profusion of bloom in Winterthur's Sundial Garden delights us, while its symmetry and repetition appeal to our sense of order.

How does one create a planting plan for a squared-off area that lacks trees, slopes, or stone outcroppings? Such was the problem H. F. du Pont faced when he decided to transform the site of his tennis courts into an April garden. Homeowners often confront a similar situation and may find inspiration in the charming arrangement known as the Sundial Garden.

The Sundial Garden is an interplay of formality and informality: beds arranged in geometric patterns create a sense of enclosure and symmetry, while any rigidity of line is softened by the profusion of bloom.

Billowing fountains of whites, pinks, and lavenders are punctuated by plants of more upright shapes and deeper tones; the perfume creates a sensuous and fairyland-like experience. Large flowering quince (*Chaenomeles* cultivars), primarily salmon-and-white Appleblossom, anchor the beds around a central armillary sundial. White spirea (*S.* x *arguta* and *S. prunifolia*) and pink flowering almond (*Prunus glandulosa*) make early appearances, as do stately magnolia trees (*M. stellata, M.* x *soulangiana*, and *M.* 'Wada's Memory') around the periphery. Several delicate Hally Jolivette cherry trees

(*Prunus* 'Hally Jolivette') bloom in misty pink, resembling confetti caught in the air. Crabapples (*Malus* cultivars) and Carolina silver bells (*Halesia carolina*) add height and color, while azaleas, viburnums, fothergillas, pearl bushes, and lilacs add to the crescendo of bloom that evokes the image of a "room made of flowers."

Du Pont's introduction of the deep purplish rose crabapple known as Henrietta Crosby (*Malus* 'Henrietta Crosby') was a masterstroke. By itself Henrietta Crosby may seem too intense, but here it is just right, adding zest to the scene. Soon lilacs bloom in their characteristic shades—lavender, pink lavender, lavender blue, white, and reddish purple, this last color sharpening and accenting the pastels. Their fragrance, along with that of several viburnums, is entrancing. *Rhododendron mucronatum* 'Amethystinum' subtly echoes the lavender shades, while the lavender spires of princess trees (*Paulownia tomentosa*) carry the banner of color across the road to Sycamore Hill.

MISE-EN-SCENE

Lilacs and bright cerise Hinode Giri azalea, with redbuds in distance.

When the Sundial Garden is blooming, harmonizing colors show up all around. A mass of bright cerise *Rhododendron* 'Hinode Giri' appears nearby, beyond which a hillside of native redbud trees (*Cercis canadensis*) provides a pinkish lavender mist. Soul mate to the redbuds, the azalea *R. reticulatum* blooms in a matching color and adds fullness to the scene.

Crabapples, viburnum, silver bell, ipheion, and spirea contribute to the feeling of being in the midst of a room made of flowers.

Green-foliage plants also play a role here. The sundial is flanked by *Ilex glabra* 'Compacta,' a cultivar of the native inkberry holly, which is repeated as an outer hedge. Low Japanese barberries (*Berberis thunbergii* 'Kobold') form inner beds. Other hollies, such as *I. crenata* 'Green Lustre,' are planted among the shrubs to separate colors and give breathing space. Later interest comes to the Sundial Garden through a white rose with single blossoms *(Rosa pimpinellifolia* var. *altaica)* and, on the outskirts, deutzias, pink spireas, and asters. Truly a feast for the senses.

Malus *'Henrietta Crosby' framed by redbud* (Cercis canadensis) *branches.*

PLANT SPECIFICS

In the Home Garden

All plants in the Sundial Garden would be good candidates for sunny places. They provide inspired color combinations and, used together, a long season of bloom. The taller shrubs, such as lilacs and viburnums, give structure and screening potential to a shrub border, while such low-mounded shrubs as Little Princess spirea and the two deutzias make good fillers for the front of a border. Most trees here are a comfortable size for the home landscape. Fothergilla and bridalwreath spirea offer fall foliage color as well.

Aster lateriflorus 'Coombe Fishacre'

ASTER
Aster
Asteraceae
Herbaceous perennial. Two cultivars described here bloom in September. They are pinched back in early summer to control height. Good cut flowers. Sun. Propagation: division or terminal cuttings.

   A. ericoides **'Pink Cloud'** (Pink Cloud aster), U.S., Mexico. Small, pink, daisy-type flowers in great numbers. Size: 3' tall, 2' spread. Soil: any good garden. Zones 5–8.
A. lateriflorus **'Coombe Fishacre'** (Coombe Fishacre aster), N. America. Fall blooming; mauve, daisy-type flowers. Size: 2'–3' tall, 3' spread. Soil: well drained. Zones 5–7.

BERBERIS THUNBERGII 'KOBOLD'
Kobold Barberry
Berberidaceae
Species: Japan; cultivar: Holland
Deciduous shrub grown for foliage. Mounds of early, rich green become deeper green in summer. Few flowers, fruits. Size: 2'–2½' tall,

Berberis thunbergii 'Kobold'

2'–3' spread. Sun. Soil: adaptable, well drained. Zones 4–8.

Cercis canadensis

CERCIS CANADENSIS
Eastern Redbud
Fabaceae
Eastern N. America
Graceful tree. Airy, pinkish lavender flowers, before leaves. Good size for home garden. Many cultivars. Prune after flowering. Size: 20'–30' tall, 25'–35' spread. Sun to light shade. Soil: many types; well drained. Propagation: softwood cuttings. Zones (3) 4–9.

CHAENOMELES CULTIVARS
Flowering Quince
For detailed information, see "Quince Walk" (page 60).

EXOCHORDA CULTIVARS
Pearl Bush
For detailed information, see "Quince Walk" (page 60).

Deutzia gracilis

DEUTZIA GRACILIS
Slender Deutzia
Saxifragaceae
Japan
Deciduous, low-spreading shrub. Upright clusters of white flowers in late May. Graceful, trouble free. Prune in early spring or after flowering. Size: 2'–4' tall, 3'–4' spread. Sun to light shade. Soil: any good garden soil, well drained. Propagation: softwood or hardwood cuttings. Zones 4–8. *D. gracilis* 'Nikko' (Nikko deutzia), low-growing, mounded shrub; white flowers in late spring. Size: 2' tall, 4' spread. Zones 5–8.

FOTHERGILLA
Fothergilla
Hamamelidaceae
Deciduous shrub. Two trouble-free, durable species native to the southeastern U.S. are grouped here. Handsome summer foliage, outstanding fall coloration, good habit. White, bottle-brush type (stamens and no petals) flowers in spring, about the same time as leaves. Sun to partial shade. Soil: moist, well drained, acid. Propagation: softwood cuttings. Two sizes. *F. gardenii* (dwarf fothergilla), many cultivars. Suckers and forms colonies. Size: 2'–4' tall, equal spread. Zones (4) 5–8 (9). *F. major* (large fothergilla), also available in many cultivars. Size: 6'–10' tall, 6'–8' spread. Zones 4–8.

HALESIA CAROLINA (TETRAPTERA)
Carolina Silver Bell
Styracaceae
Southeastern U.S.
Deciduous tree. White, bell-shape flowers in midspring, before or with leaves. Pest free. Propagation: softwood cuttings. Prune after flowering. Size: 30'–40' tall, 20'–35' spread. Sun to partial shade. Soil: moist, well drained, acid. Zones 4–8 (9).

ILEX
Holly
Aquifoliaceae
The two cultivars grouped here are grown for lustrous evergreen foliage. Propagation: softwood cuttings. *I. crenata* 'Green Lustre' (Green Lustre holly), species from Japan. Rounded shrub; small, leathery, green leaves. Many other cultivars. Size: 3'–4' tall, 6'–8' spread. Sun or shade. Soil: moist, well drained, slightly acid. Zones 5–7. *I. glabra*

Ilex glabra 'Compacta'

'Compacta' (dwarf inkberry holly), species from eastern N. America. Rather upright shrub; small, glossy leaves. Problem free. Many other cultivars. Size: 4'–6' tall, equal spread. Sun or shade. Soil: acid, can be damp; adaptable. Zones 4–9.

MAGNOLIA
SPECIES AND CULTIVARS
For detailed information, see "Magnolia Bend" (page 53).

MALUS
CULTIVARS
Crabapple Cultivars
Rosaceae
Species: N. America, Europe, Asia
Deciduous trees. Innumerable cultivars; species hybridize freely. Flowers range from white to pink to purple-rose; bloom with leaves in midspring. All have interesting fruits in red, yellow, or green shades. (Apples, with larger fruits, are also in this genus.) Propagation: softwood cuttings. Prune soon after flowering. *M.* 'Henrietta Crosby' and *M.* 'Adams,' deep purplish rose flowers; *M.* x *atrosanguinea*, purplish rose;

Branch of Malus 'Henrietta Crosby'

M. halliana **'Parkmanii,'** rose turning pink. Size: 15'–30' tall, equal spread. Sun. Soil: moist, well drained, acid. Zones (3) 4–8.

Paulownia tomentosa

PAULOWNIA TOMENTOSA
Princess Tree
Scrophulariaceae
China

Deciduous tree. Lavender blossoms held in pyramidal clusters in midspring, as leaves emerge. Propagation: seeds. Prune in winter. Size: 30'–40' tall, equal spread. Sun to partial shade. Soil: moist, well drained. Zones 5–9.

Prunus 'Hally Jolivette'

PRUNUS
Rosaceae
Genus includes cherries, peaches, apricots, plums, almonds. Included here are a deciduous shrub and a tree. Propagation: softwood cuttings. Prune after flowering.

Sun. Soil: any good garden.

P. glandulosa (dwarf flowering almond), China. Leafless branches covered with puffs of pink flowers in early spring. Very decorative; may be short lived. Size: 4'–5' tall, equal spread. Zones 4–8. *P.* **'Hally Jolivette'** (Hally Jolivette cherry), parents from Japan. Rounded tree or shrub. Pink buds become almost white, double flowers preceding the leaves. Flowers over a long period in early spring. Branches to the ground. Size: 15'–20' tall, equal spread. Zones 5–7.

RHODODENDRON
Azaleas and Rhododendrons
Ericaceae
Early- and midspring azaleas and rhododendrons are found in the Sundial Garden. For more information, see "Other Noteworthy Azaleas and Rhododendrons" (page 77). Soil: acid, moist, well drained, high organic content. Partial shade unless otherwise noted.

Early-season cultivars: *R.* 'Conewago' and *R.* 'Conewago Improved,' semi-evergreen shrubs. Pinkish lavender, ball-shape trusses early in spring. Size: 4'–6' tall, 3'–5' spread. Sun to partial shade. Zones (4) 5–8. *R. chapmanii* 'Wonder,' evergreen shrub. Lavender

Rhododendron mucronatum 'Amethystinum'

Rhododendron reticulatum

pink flowers, held in compact trusses, in early spring. Size: 4' tall, 4' spread. Sun to partial shade. Zones (5) 6–8.

Midseason cultivars: *R. mucronatum* 'Amethystinum' (Amethystinum azalea), palest lavender flowers. Size: 6' tall, 6'–8' spread. Zones 6–9. Nearby midseason cultivars : *R.* 'Hinode Giri' (Hinode Giri Kurume azalea), a compact evergreen azalea with cerise flowers. Size: 3' tall, equal spread. Zones 6–8 (9). *R. reticulatum*, an upright-growing deciduous azalea; pinkish lavender, funnel-form flowers precede leaves. Size: 6' tall, 6' spread. Sun or part shade. Zones 6–8.

ROSA PIMPINELLIFOLIA VAR. ALTAICA
Scotch Rose
Rosaceae
Europe, Asia

Shrub of easy culture but very thorny. White, single blossoms in early summer. Will sucker and form thickets. Size: 3'–4' tall, equal spread. Soil: well drained, sandy. Sun. Zones 4–8.

Spiraea japonica 'Little Princess'

SPIRAEA
Spirea
Rosaceae

Deciduous shrubs; adaptable, trouble free. White or pink flowers. Some types bloom in spring, others in early summer. Propagation: softwood or hardwood cuttings. Prune after flowering. Soil: any good garden.

S. **x arguta** (garland spirea), parents from Europe, Asia. Delicate white blossoms cover arching branches in early spring, before leaves. Similar to *S. thunbergii*. Size: 3'–6' tall, equal spread. Sun to partial shade. Zones 4–8. *S. japonica* **'Little Princess'** (Little Princess spirea), cultivar from Holland. Low, mounded shrub.

Flowers in slightly rounded, pink clusters; long summer flowering. May be pruned in early spring. Size: 2'–3' tall, equal spread. Sun to partial shade. Zones 4–8. *S. prunifolia* (bridalwreath spirea), Asia. Double white, buttonlike flowers cover outstretched branches in early spring. Apricot-colored fall foliage. Size: 4'–9' tall, 6'–8' spread. Sun. Zones 4–8.

SYRINGA
Lilac
Oleaceae
Europe

Two similar lilacs are grouped here. Deciduous, vase-shape shrubs; arching branches. Fragrant flowers form pyramidal clusters. Innumerable cultivars in many colors, most blend well. Deadheading desirable but not necessary. Prune soon after flowering by removing largest canes near ground level. Propagation: softwood cuttings. Size: 8'–15' tall, 6'–15' spread. Soil: neutral, pH adaptable, well drained. Sun. Zones 3–7 (8).

Syringa vulgaris (common lilac), Europe. Noteworthy cultivars in the Sundial Garden are 'Mme. Charles Souchet,' lavender blue; 'Wedgwood Blue,' lavender blue; 'Priscilla,' lavender mauve; 'Katherine

Syringa vulgaris 'Priscilla'

Havemeyer,' pink; 'Maud Notcutt,' large, white; 'Primrose,' pale yellow.

S. x hyacinthiflora (*S. oblata* x *S. vulgaris*; early-flowering lilac), parents from Korea and Europe. Similar to *S. vulgaris* but slightly larger, more vigorous, hardier, and earlier blooming. Representatives in the Sundial Garden include 'Assessippi,' lavender; 'Clarke's Giant,' large, lavender blue.

VIBURNUM
Viburnum
Caprifoliaceae

Easy and dependable; some of the most useful plants for the home garden. Species and cultivars (except *V. macrocephalum*) in or near the Sundial Garden have pink buds in spring that open as rounded clusters of white flowers noted for their fragrance. Many cultivars. Prune after flowering. Soil: moist, well drained, slightly acid. Propagation: softwood cuttings.

V. x burkwoodii (burkwood viburnum), parents from Asia. Large, vigorous shrub; evergreen in warm climates. Flower clusters of 2"–3". Sun. Size: 8'–10' tall, 5'–7' spread. Zones (4) 5–8. *V. carlesii* (Koreanspice viburnum), Korea. Deciduous shrub, 2"–3" flower clusters. Much loved for its fragrance. Size: 4'–8' tall, equal spread. Sun to partial shade. Zones 4–7 (8). *V. x carlcephalum* (fragrant viburnum), parents from Asia. Deciduous; 5" flower clusters. Size: 6'–10' tall, equal spread. Sun. Zones (5) 6–8. *V. x juddii* (Judd viburnum), parents from Asia. Deciduous; 2"–3" flower clusters; somewhat more disease resistant than *V. carlesii*. Size: 6'–8' tall, equal spread. Sun. Zones 4–8. *V. macrocephalum* (Chinese snowball viburnum), China. Deciduous to semi-evergreen large-scale shrub, spectacular in bloom. Size: 10'–20' tall, equal spread. Sun to partial shade. Zones 6–9.

TWO OLD FRIENDS

Contemplating a new April garden in 1955, H. F. du Pont asked Marian Cruger Coffin, a landscape architect and lifelong friend, to suggest a design. They had collaborated on many garden projects through the years and, although Coffin was unwell, she accepted the invitation with alacrity. Together they developed the Sundial Garden—Coffin was responsible for the project's graceful geometric patterns, du Pont the plant selection. Many people feel that this collaboration, their last, is their finest.

AZALEA WOODS
April–May

The play of dappled sunlight is part of the charm of Winterthur's Azalea Woods.

The highlight of the azalea season is unquestionably the full flowering of eight-acre Azalea Woods in early May. Started as a small nursery in 1917, this area has grown into a famous showplace whose bloom time is, for many, their favorite time to visit Winterthur.

In the shelter of old-forest trees, clouds of white dogwood blossoms *(Cornus florida)* seem to float in the air. Below these, azaleas produce waves of color and are soon joined by soft or deeply colored broadleaf rhododendrons. A medley of wildflowers and ferns covers the woodland floor.

Surprisingly few azalea cultivars—mostly Kurumes—make up the vast Azalea Woods. Du Pont planted large masses of each cultivar and repeated his

72

favorites in several places. He juxtaposed harmonious pastels; combined lighter and darker shades of the same color; blended textures of the same color (two whites, for example); and in some cases mixed two colors, near discords, that make us look twice. When asked about these unusual combinations, such as lavender and cherry red, du Pont replied that they would "chic it up." Along several paths, giant broad-leaved evergreen rhododendrons produce spectacular displays of huge, delicately colored trusses. The masterstroke, however, was underplanting the entire garden with thousands of brilliant Spanish bluebells *(Hyacinthoides hispanica)*, which counterpoint the reds, pinks, corals, lavenders, and whites of the shrubs and cause the woods to come alive.

The principal forest trees that populate Azalea Woods include oaks *(Quercus* species), tulip-poplars, American beech, and hickories. Wildflowers include trilliums *(Trillium grandiflorum)*, Jacob's ladder *(Polemonium reptans)*, primulas *(Primula elatior)*, wild geranium *(Geranium maculatum)*, dame's rocket *(Hesperis matronalis)*, and silvery glade fern *(Athyrium thelypterioides)*. Native plants, Japanese azaleas, hybrid rhododendrons, and Spanish bluebells all look per-fectly at home in this American woodland garden.

"Art is the achievement of unity in diversity," wrote Will Durant. Here, hybrid rhododendrons, Spanish bluebells, and naturalized dame's rocket commingle.

PATHS

Paths are a great asset when designing a landscape. In a large garden, they invite us in and, as they curve along to a point out of sight, pique our curiosity about what lies beyond. As we stroll, the garden is presented as a series of scenes or views. In small-

er gardens, paths direct our eyes and help us make sense of the design of which they form an important element. Paths, of course, also provide use-ful access to plants for maintenance.

In the Home Garden

You may wonder how to transfer the concepts in Azalea Woods to your own yard. A large tree or, better still, a group of two or three can present a starting point. Oaks are ideal in supplying the necessary acidic soil (see Quercus rubra *on page 75), but other deciduous trees will work. In their shelter, you might plant one or two white dogwoods and a few May-blooming azaleas (probably Kurumes) in soft tones and underplant the area with Spanish bluebells. Such a plan is horticulturally feasible since dogwoods grow naturally at the edge of woods, liking some shelter but also sunlight and air. The azaleas will appreciate the shade of the trees, and Spanish bluebells will bloom in sun or shade at the time of the azaleas. You can even add a few trilliums, wild geraniums, primulas, or ferns to carry out the theme in your Azalea Woods "lite."*

ATHYRIUM THELYPTERIOIDES
Silvery Glade Fern
Polypodiaceae
Eastern U.S.

Light green, lacy fronds. Spreads. Propagation: division. Size: 2'–3' tall, equal spread. Soil: moist, rich in humus, or moist sandy. Shade to partial shade. Zones 4–8.

CORNUS FLORIDA
Flowering Dogwood
Cornaceae
Eastern U.S. and Mexico

Deciduous tree; beautiful horizontal branching habit. In early spring, showy white bracts surround the true flowers, helping make this an all-time favorite native tree. Excellent fall foliage, fruit. Innumerable cultivars. Propagation: softwood cuttings. Size: 20'–40' tall, equal spread. Soil: acid, moist, well drained, high organic. Partial shade to full sun. Zones (5) 6–9.

GERANIUM MACULATUM
Wild Geranium
Geraniaceae
Eastern N. America

Geranium maculatum

Herbaceous perennial. Rose lavender flowers arise in spring from a clump of palmately lobed leaves. Sometimes called cranesbill because of seedpod shape. Propagation: seed, division. Size: 12"–20" tall, equal spread. Soil: moist, acid to neutral. Sun to partial shade. Zones 3–8 (9).

HESPERIS MATRONALIS
Dame's Rocket
Brassicaceae

For detailed information, see "Wildflowers of Spring" (page 47).

Hyacinthoides hispanica

HYACINTHOIDES HISPANICA
Spanish Bluebells
Liliaceae
Europe, N. Africa

Bulb. Bells of rich lavender-blue in mid-spring; stems arise from a clump of straplike leaves. Cultivars available. Propagation: division of clumps in fall, seeds. Size: 12"–15" tall, 12" spread. Soil: well drained. Sun to partial or deeper shade. Zones 4–7.

Polemonium reptans

POLEMONIUM REPTANS
Jacob's Ladder
Polemoniaceae
Eastern N. America
Herbaceous perennial. Attractive foliage
resembles a ladder. Soft blue flowers bloom
in midspring. Naturalizes. Propagation: seed
and division. Size: 8"–18" tall, 12"–14" spread.
Soil: moist, humus rich. Partial shade.
Zones (2) 3–7 (8).

PRIMULA ELATIOR
Oxlip Primrose
Primulaceae
Europe
Herbaceous perennial. Clusters of nodding,
pale yellow flowers on stems that arise from

Primula elatior

a clump of green leaves in early spring.
Propagation: division, seed. Size: 8" tall,
equal spread. Soil: moist, humus rich. Partial
shade. Zone 5–7.

QUERCUS RUBRA
Red Oak
Fagaceae
Northern and Eastern U.S. and Canada
Deciduous, fast-growing, trouble-free tree;
easily transplanted. Good choice for home
gardeners desiring a sheltering tree for
azaleas or rhododendrons. Propagation: seed.
Size: 60'–75' tall, nearly equal spread.
Soil: well drained, light, slightly acid. Sun.
Zones 4–7 (8).

RHODODENDRON
Rhododendron
Ericaceae
Grouped here are some Kurume azaleas
and large-leaved, evergreen rhododendron
cultivars. Individual cultivars vary in
adaptability to geographic/floristic regions
and hardiness. Great strides have been made
in hybridizing for heat/cold hardiness and
other attributes. Consult catalogues for plants
recommended for your area. Soil: acid,

Rhododendron 'Early Pink #1'

rich organic, moist, well drained. Partial shade.
See "Other Noteworthy Azaleas and
Rhododendrons" (page 77) for pruning
and propagation information.

Note: Taxonomists classify azaleas botanically
as rhododendrons, so you will find Kurume
azaleas listed under Rhododendron. In
practice, however, gardeners and tradespeople
routinely call certain plants azaleas and others
rhododendrons (as in this book). In general,
azaleas are shrubs with many individual
blossoms and small leaves, whereas rhododendrons are shrubs with blossoms in trusses and
whorls of large evergreen leaves. Furthermore,
azaleas have five stamens and funnel-form
blossoms; rhododendrons have ten or more

stamens and bell-shape blossoms. But there are many exceptions. Nature is complex, and the division is imperfect in the classification of the nine hundred or so species of rhododendrons and countless hybrids.

KURUME HYBRIDS
Japan
Evergreen, spreading shrubs covered with funnel-form blossoms in midspring. Small, dark green leaves; flowers in many colors— whites through pinks, corals, lavenders to reds. Although some Kurumes in Azalea Woods are known only by du Pont's identifying numbers, substitutes are available. For example, his #10 is similar to 'Blaauw's Pink,' a salmon pink hose-in-hose. Named cultivars in Azalea Woods include **'Pink Pearl,'** luminescent hose-in-hose, pink with light centers; **'Apple Blossom,'** light pink single with glossy leaves; **'Snow,'** vigorous, white hose-in-hose; **'Rose Greeley,'** fragrant, white hose-in-hose (Gable hybrid); **'Lavender Queen,'** free-flowering, light lavender single; **'Mauve**

Beauty,' free-flowering, mauve hose-in-hose; and **'Arnoldiana'** (*R. obtusum amoenum* x *kaempferi* 'Arnoldiana'), cherry red. All range in size from 3' to 8' tall, 4'–10' spread. Zones 6–8 (9).

LARGE-LEAVED EVERGREEN RHODODENDRON CULTIVARS
Parentage varies
Excellent here and available in the trade: **'Ben Moseley,'** a light purplish pink with dark blotch; **'County of York,'** upright white trusses of good substance and heat resistance; **'Goldfort,'** light yellow, adaptable; **'Janet Blair,'** delicate, frilled, pink flowers, easy to grow, widely adapted; **'Scintillation,'** pink, excellent flowers, foliage, and habit—deservedly popular; **'Skyglow,'** peach colored, edged pink, greenish blotch. Du Pont's "cherry red" rhododendron, which figures prominently in Azalea Woods, is known only as Dexter #11. It is similar to 'Wissahickon,' a Dexter hybrid available in the trade. All range in size from 5' to 6' tall, equal spread. Zones 5–9 (10).

Trillium grandiflorum

TRILLIUM GRANDIFLORUM
Great White Trillium
Liliaceae
Eastern N. America
Herbaceous perennial. Upright stems carry three leaves and white, three-petaled flowers in spring. Flowers slowly turn pink. Propagation: division in early fall. Many other species of trillium, some rare, grow in the woodlands here. Size: 18"–24" tall, 12"–18" spread. Soil: moist, well drained. Partial shade. Zones (3) 4–7 (8).

AN AMAZING GENUS
Rhododendron is a genus that comprises more than 900 species, the great majority of which are native to the mountains of Asia. Gardeners are fortunate that many species and hybrids will grow in various locales and that further hybridizing for adaptability and other traits continues. North America also has native rhododendrons and azaleas. These have been used as components in the creation of exciting races and are still undergoing hybridization and selection.

OTHER NOTEWORTHY AZALEAS AND RHODODENDRONS
April–July

Azaleas are truly the backbone of Winterthur's spring garden, blooming from early April until late July. "No other plant," said du Pont, "will give four months of bloom in Delaware." He capitalized on this bounty, repeating favorites in several areas, thus giving unity to the garden through echoing colors and recurring motifs. Many of these good growers fall naturally into other sections of this book. Included here are additional plants of value to the home gardener.

In late April and early May, the evergreens of the Pinetum are illumined by an all-time favorite, the royal

The hybrid Miss Susie adds a bright pink note to Winterthur's Pinetum in early May.

azalea *(R. schlippenbachii)*. This tall, deciduous shrub features large, soft pink blossoms that have been likened to alighting butterflies. Other azaleas here continue the pink theme, including the Wheeldon hybrid Miss Susie. Glenn Dale hybrids (namely, Ambrosia, a deep salmon) and several Chisholm Merritt hybrids (including Millicent and Flower Queen) fill the Pinetum with color in early May.

Later in the month, snow azalea *(R. mucronatum)* and some of its cultivars bloom. In the Sundial Garden, large, white, single flowers of snow azalea appear near the lavender-tinted cultivar Amethystinum. The white, strawberry-throated cultivar Magnifica blooms at Magnolia Bend, in Azalea Woods, and in the Peony

Rhododendron mucronatum *'Winterthur' blooms beside the Forbidden Fairy Ring in Enchanted Woods.*™

Garden. Magnifica often puts out "sports," branches whose flower color differs from the rest of the plant. One such sport, a soft lavender with lovely fragrance, was special enough to be propagated here and given the name Winterthur. Large plantings of this azalea appear in Enchanted Woods™, on Oak Hill, and at the Reflecting Pool.

In early June along Clenny Run, magnificent rosebay rhododendron hybrids (*R. maximum* hybrids) bloom in soft shades of lavender and pink. True to their name, they are enormous, stately, and spectacular and would be outstanding for a large site. Deep pink azalea J. T. Lovett, an indicum cultivar, adds a bright accent. Also blooming in June and of indicum parentage is a striking coral-colored hybrid whose name Beni Kirishima denotes its Japanese origins. It grows happily in the dappled shade of Oak Hill. A third June bloomer with indicum parentage is *R.* 'Balsaminaeflorum,' a diminutive azalea with distinctive, rosebudlike blossoms in a soft salmon shade. Found on the March Bank and at Magnolia Bend, this old favorite is valuable as a vigorous grower that stays low and would be nice for a rock garden or a ground-cover planting.

Throughout spring, native azaleas bloom on Oak Hill. These deciduous plants with honeysuckle-like blossoms (they are sometimes called bush honeysuckle) come in colors that recall fruit sherbets. Two early-blooming pinks are the delicate pinxterbloom *(R. pericly-menoides)* and the highly rated pinkshell azalea *(R. vaseyi)*. Sweet-smelling coast azalea *(R. atlanticum)*, an excellent white, blooms in May. In June white Alabama azalea

A group of native azaleas blooms on Winterthur's Oak Hill. Their honeysuckle-like blossoms come in fruit sherbet colors.

(R. alabamense) appears, flame azalea *(R. calendulaceum)* colors the woods in orange, yellow, and red tones; and, a week or two later, Cumberland azalea *(R. bakeri)* flowers in reddish orange. In July and August, a large planting of coral-colored plum-leaf azalea *(R. prunifolium)* brightens a hillside above the Quarry Garden. As these native azaleas have become better known, various cultivars with special properties have been selected and are available in the trade. Hybridizers in Europe have used the American species as parents of many delightful deciduous hybrids, such as Ghent and Exbury azaleas.

Many other species, hybrids, and cultivars appear in smaller numbers throughout the garden and are labeled. Visitors to Winterthur, connoisseur and beginning gardener alike, will find many wonderful plants to enjoy.

In the Home Garden

Large-leaved evergreen rhodo-
dendrons, with their huge trusses, are
the epitome of elegance and add
enormously to any garden. Their grand
scale requires the accompaniment
of large trees or tall buildings. They
look appropriate and comfortable
in woodland settings, under deciduous
trees in island beds, or with pines or
other conifers. Small-leaved rhododen-
drons and evergreen azaleas are easier
to incorporate into plantings around
the foundation of a home, and they
can also tolerate more sun. Deciduous
azaleas, being rather informal,
add both grace and delicacy to a wood-
land setting; they also provide variety
and color to a shrub border, island bed,
or conifer collection. Most rhododen-
drons and azaleas look their best and
grow well in dappled shade.

RHODODENDRON
Rhododendron
Ericaceae

Grouped here is a selection of evergreen and deciduous rhododendrons and azaleas. (The term *evergreen* in this context is only an approximation; evergreen azaleas are more accurately called persistent leaved. Many have two sets of leaves: spring leaves often drop in the fall; summer leaves may remain during the winter, depending mostly on climate.)

Pruning large-leaved rhododendrons: preferably in early spring, cut back to one of the recent rosettes of leaves, cutting about one-quarter inch above the rosette. If more drastic pruning is needed as a rejuvenation, about one-third of the growth should be removed yearly for three years. Pruning small-leaved rhododendrons, evergreen azaleas, and deciduous azaleas: after flowering, cut anywhere along the branch. Best to reach down into the shrub when cutting so that the stub is covered by other branches. Propagation of large-leaved evergreen rhododendrons: cuttings taken after new growth shows firmness. Propagation of evergreen azaleas: softwood cuttings taken in summer. Propagation of deciduous azaleas: softwood cuttings taken early in the season. Soil (for all): acid, moist, well drained, organic. Partial shade.

DECIDUOUS AZALEAS

Here is a selection of deciduous azaleas native to the eastern United States, followed by one deciduous Asiatic azalea. **R. alabamense** (Alabama azalea), AL, GA. White, fragrant flowers, in clusters of 6–10, open with the leaves in early summer. Size: 5'–6' tall, 8' spread. Zones 7–8. **R. atlanticum** (coast azalea), DE to SC. White flowers, often with pink tube, open with the leaves in late spring. Blue-green foliage. Stoloniferous. Cultivars available. Size: 3'–6' tall, equal spread. Zones 5–8 (9). **R. bakeri** (Cumberland azalea), KY to GA. Orange to red funnel-form flowers open in early summer, after the leaves. Size: 3'–8' tall, equal spread. Zones 5–7. **R. calendulaceum**

R. calendulaceum

(flame azalea), PA to GA. Upright shrub. Funnel-form flowers in yellow, orange, or red open with or after the leaves in early summer. Many cultivars. Size: 6'–10' tall, equal spread. Zones 5–7. **R. periclymenoides** (pinxterbloom azalea), MA to NC. Clusters of delicate, pink flowers in early spring, before leaves. Stoloniferous. Tolerates dry soil. Size: 4'–6' tall, equal spread (yet quite variable). Zones (3) 4–8. **R. prunifolium** (plum-leaf azalea), GA, AL. Large, spreading shrub. Orange-red flowers in July. Cuttings root readily. Cultivars available. Size: 8'–10' tall, equal spread. Zones 5–8 (9). **R. vaseyi** (pinkshell azalea), NC. Clusters of rose-colored flowers in early spring, before leaves. Tolerates moist conditions. Good reddish fall color. Cultivar 'White Find' is highly rated. Size: 5'–10' tall, equal spread. Zones 4–7 (8).

R. schlippenbachii

R. indicum 'Balsaminaeflorum'

R. mucronatum

R. schlippenbachii (royal azalea), Korea, Manchuria. Upright shrub. Delicate pink flowers with flaring petals. Midspring. Broad, rounded leaves, seemingly arranged in whorls, appear with or just after the flowers. Size: 6'–8' tall, equal spread. Zones 4–7.

EVERGREEN AZALEAS

Four evergreen azaleas in the Pinetum offer pink flowers and midspring bloom. (If these are hard to find, 'Blauuw's Pink,' a dependable, salmon hose-in-hose, may be substituted for any. Size: 5' tall, equal spread. Zones 6–8 [9].) **'Ambrosia,'** Glenn Dale introduction; large, salmon pink flowers. Size: 8' tall, equal spread. Zones 6–9. **'Flower Queen,'** Chisholm Merritt introduction; pink. Size: 5' tall, equal spread. Zones 7–9. **'Millicent,'** a Chisholm Merritt introduction; pink. Size: 5' tall, equal spread. Zones 7–9. **'Miss Susie,'** Wheeldon introduction; bright pink. Size: 5'–6' tall, equal spread. Zones 7–9.

R. INDICUM CULTIVARS

Cultivars of *R. indicum*, a Japanese, late-blooming species: All evergreen, low growing, and bloom in early summer.

'Balsaminaeflorum,' salmon pink, rosebud-type flowers. Easy. Size: 1'–3' tall, equal spread. Zones (6) 7–9. **'Beni Kirishima,'**

R. indicum 'Beni Kirishima'

coral, funnel-form, double flowers. Size: 4' tall, equal spread. Zones 7–10. **'J. T. Lovett,'** deep pink, funnel-form flowers. Size: 3' tall, equal spread. Zones 7–10.

R. MUCRONATUM AND CULTIVARS

R. mucronatum and cultivars: **R. mucronatum** (snow azalea), Japan. Spreading evergreen shrub. Large, pure white flowers in late spring. Sometimes listed as *R. ledifolium.* Substitute could be 'Delaware Valley White,'

a derivative (3' tall). Cultivars: 'Amethystinum,' palest lavender; 'Magnifica,' white with strawberry throat; and 'Winterthur,' fragrant lavender flowers. Size (for all): 6' tall, 6'–8' spread. Zones 6–9.

EVERGREEN RHODODENDRONS

R. MAXIMUM HYBRIDS
Rosebay Rhododendron Hybrids
Species: Eastern U.S.
Huge shrubs. Handsome, lavender and pinkish lavender trusses in early summer. Cold hardy. Appreciate cool conditions. Size: 12'–30' tall, equal spread. Zones 3–7.

R. maximum hybrids at Clenny Run

"I have a little stream fenced
off from my Holsteins for my
Japonicas [primulas], and a very
recent bog garden which never
dries in our hot summers, where
I am featuring the candelabras
[primulas] for the benefit of
the many visitors who come
to our gardens."

— H. F. du Pont, 1963

$\mathcal{S}$pring into Summer

*"You can't make a silk purse
out of a sow's ear."*

—*Jonathan Swift,* Polite Conversation, *about 1725*

Undeterred by Jonathan Swift's oft-quoted thought, H. F. du Pont
did just that when he created his May-blooming Quarry Garden.
The transformation of a problem area into an idyllic rock garden is
described in the pages that follow. Two other areas at Winterthur share
the stage at this season: The Peony Garden features superb yet practical
plants, and Sycamore Hill presents Asiatic plants as well as handsome
native trees and shrubs. Three unique gardens are presented here
for your pleasure and inspiration.

Opener: Winterthur's Sycamore Hill, sometimes referred to as the June garden,
offers late lilacs, deutzia, kousa dogwoods, and other spring-into-summer plants
in pleasing combinations.

Left: Saunders peonies are well represented in Winterthur's Peony Garden.

QUARRY GARDEN
May–August

Rhododendron kiusianum *blooms beside steps that invite visitors into the heart of Winterthur's Quarry Garden.*

In 1962 H. F. du Pont transformed an abandoned stone quarry into a romantic garden, a remarkable demonstration of his talent for seeing the potential of a site and realizing it. The landscaping of surrounding areas had begun to encroach upon this open pit, and du Pont had long wished for a damp location where he could grow primulas. With notable ingenuity, he created the massive rock garden that we know today as the Quarry Garden.

Visitors can look down upon the Quarry Garden from several vantage points. Better yet, garden-goers can wander down into it on steps that descend as though into a deep bowl. Trailing shrubs, ferns, and other herbaceous plants spill out of crevices in stone walls. Paths and places to sit appear at lower levels, while the lowest level is boglike. There, springs feed three gentle streams that meander along the garden floor, creating ideal conditions for moisture-loving primulas, iris, and other bog plants.

Two rhododendrons bloom here in mid May, giving promise of the color soon to unfold on the quarry floor. Flanking the steps, diminutive *R. kiusianum* flowers in lavender, while along the walls, *R.* x *mortieri* blossoms in soft coral. In late May, the garden floor becomes a quilt of candelabra primulas (*Primula* species and a hybrid), or primroses. Blooming in unusual, muted colors—plum, apricot, coral, gold, lavender pink—their subtle shades blend beautifully. These primulas are characterized by blossoms clustered around the stem in whorls arranged in tiers, hence the name *candelabra*. The blossoms open one tier after another, resulting in a long bloom period. A shady streamside in the home garden would be ideal for these plants. In any situation, however, they must be kept moist during the summer.

Another candelabra found at Winterthur is Japanese primrose (*P. japonica*), which comes in reds, pinks, whites, and mixtures of these colors. It pops up along various streams on the estate. This primrose is easy to grow, aggressive, and tends to crowd out shyer candelabras; therefore, it is not allowed to become established in the Quarry Garden. Off by itself, however, it is perfectly lovely.

Irises growing here are also adapted to wet conditions. These plants introduce yellow, lavender, purple, and white to the color scheme, and some have variegated leaves with cream and green striations. The rocks,

crevices, and shade make an ideal setting for various naturalized plants as well. Among them is the delicate fern-leaf corydalis (*Corydalis cheilanthifolia*), whose yellow flowers appear in April, and handsome bearsfoot hellebore (*Helleborus foetidus*), which offers greenish blossoms during a long period in spring as well as new leaves in late May.

In July and August, lobelias attract butterflies and birds. The bright red spires of the cardinal flower (*Lobelia cardinalis*) are likely their favorites, certainly of the hummingbirds. Yet another handsome, tall specimen is big blue lobelia (*Lobelia siphilitica*), which is a delightful

Lobelia siphilitica *blooms in the Quarry Garden and nearby.*

shade of purple. (As gardeners know, true blue is uncommon in the horticultural world, and purple and lavender plants are often called blue.) These lobelias and others are the parents of various hybrids, resulting in a range of colors—including rose, lavender, purple, and white—that offer good choices for the moist, shady garden.

Meanwhile, a member of the great genus clematis flourishes on a slightly drier bank nearby. Tube clematis (*Clematis heracleifolia* var. *davidiana*) is much prettier than its common name suggests. The fragrant blossoms of this sprawling subshrub are reminiscent of hyacinths; the soft blue blooms appear in late August and are a fine addition to the late-summer garden.

Candelabra primulas in soft, muted tones carpet the moist quarry floor.

PLANT SPECIFICS

In the Home Garden

*If you have a semishady, damp spot —
perhaps even a problem area — any
or all of the interesting plants described
here are worth a try. Some of the
delightful primulas offer a starting
place. If you want a plant that
will take care of itself, given the right
conditions,* Primula japonica
*can be quite carefree.
Some of these plants do not need bog
conditions. Lobelias, for instance, are
easy to grow in ordinary garden soil.*
Clematis heracleifolia *is an
appealing, sprawling shrub of lovely
color that appears in late summer
when our gardens may need a lift.
And fern-leaf corydalis is ideal for
crevices in a shady stone wall.*

Clematis heracleifolia var. *davidiana*

CLEMATIS HERACLEIFOLIA VAR. DAVIDIANA
Tube Clematis
Ranunculaceae
China
Deciduous, sprawling subshrub. Blue,
hyacinth-like flowers in late summer.
Prune in spring. Propagation: self-sows or
by terminal cuttings in summer. Size: 2'–3'
tall, 3' spread. Soil: moist but not boglike.
Sun. Zones 3–7.

Corydalis cheilanthifolia

CORYDALIS CHEILANTHIFOLIA
Fern-Leaf Corydalis
Fumariaceae
China
Herbaceous perennial. Ferny foliage. Yellow
flowers with turned-up spurs along upright
stems in early spring. Propagation: self-sows
or division. Size: 9"–12" tall, 12" spread.
Soil: rock crevices seem ideal; well-drained,
good garden soil. Partial shade to shade.
Zones 3–6.

Helleborus foetidus

HELLEBORUS FOETIDUS
Bearsfoot Hellebore
Ranunculaceae
Europe

Herbaceous perennial; semi-evergreen.
Light green, cup-shape blossoms on ends of
branched stems. Narrow, leathery, palmate
leaves. Division of clumps not advised but
self-sows. Size: 18"–24" tall, 18" spread.
Soil: moist, well drained is best but tolerates
heavier; slightly alkaline. Partial shade.
Zones 5–7 (8).

Iris ensata

IRIS
Iris
Iridaceae

Herbaceous perennial. Delicate flowers
composed of three outer segments (falls),
three inner segments (standards). Irises for
damp or wet places are described here.
Propagation: division. Soil: moist, acid, rich
organic. Sun or partial shade.

   I. ensata, formerly *I. kaempferi*
(Japanese iris), Japan, China. Large falls
held horizontally, with almost no standards,
create an exotic, regal look. Blooms in early
summer. Does not need bog conditions.
Size: 24"–30" tall, 24" spread. Zones 4–9.
I. laevigata **'Variegata'** (rabbit-ear iris),
species from Japan. Variegated foliage; purple,
flattened flowers in early summer. Bog plant,
but tolerant of nonacidic soils. Other cultivars
available. Size: 2' tall, equal spread. Zones
4–9. *I. hexagona* (Dixie iris), South Carolina
to Gulf states. One of the so-called Louisiana
iris native to the Gulf region. Purple flowers
with yellow markings in late spring. Grows
in swamps. Many cultivars. Size: 2'–3' tall, 2'
spread. Zones 4–9. *I. pseudacorus* (yellow
flag), Europe; naturalized in eastern U.S.

Yellow falls with lighter standards in late
spring. Bladelike leaves, elegant buds.
Will grow in water, bogs, or drier situations
if additional water provided. Many cultivars.
Size: 2'–3' tall, 2' spread. Zones 5–9.
I. pseudacorus **'Variegata,'** *I. pseudacorus* with
variegated foliage.

Lobelia siphilitica

LOBELIA
Lobelia
Campanulaceae

Two colorful species native to North America
as well as a hybrid are described here.
Midsummer bloom. Flowers bloom from
bottom to top along tall stems. Though not

true perennials, each develops offsets that quickly root. Propagation: seed or division (species); division (cultivars). Soil: moist, humus rich; will stand wet. Shade in South, shade to sun in North.

L. cardinalis (cardinal flower), brilliant red flowers attract hummingbirds. Self-sows. Size: 2'–4' tall, 1' spread. Zones (2) 3–9. *L. siphilitica* (big blue lobelia), flowers in a lovely purple shade. Self-sows. Size: 2'–3' tall, 1' spread. Zones (3) 4–8 (9). *L. x speciosa* **'Rose Beacon'** (Rose Beacon lobelia), rose colored. Size: 2'–3' tall, 1' spread. Zones 5–8.

Primula japonica

PRIMULA
Primrose
Primulaceae

Herbaceous perennials. Whorls of flowers in tiers around strong stems. Some hybrids are easier to grow than the species. Wide range of interesting colors. Late-spring bloom. Propagation: from seed (species); division after flowering (cultivars). Soil: consistently moist, well drained, high organic. Partial shade (unless otherwise noted).

Candelabra Primroses: *P. beesiana* (bees primrose), China. Lavender pink. Size: 18"–24"

tall, 24" spread. Zones 6–8. *P. x bullesiana* (bulles primrose), parents from China. Cream, orange, pink, red, and purple. Size: 2' tall, equal spread. Full sun in the north. Zones (5) 6–7 (8). *P. bulleyana* (bulley's primrose), China. Orange-yellow. Size: 2'–3' tall, equal spread. Zones 6–8. *P. burmanica* (burman primrose), Burma. Reddish purple. Size: 2' tall, equal spread. Zones 6–8. *P. japonica* (Japanese primrose), Japan. Red, pink, white, purple as well as mixtures present in many plantings due to self-seeding. Aggressive; crowds out other candelabras. Cultivars available. Size: 12"–24" tall, 24" spread. Zones 5–7. *P. pulverulenta* (silverdust primrose), China. Reddish purple. Easily grown. 'Bartley's Strain,' is a soft pink cultivar. Size: 30" tall, equal spread. Zones 5–8.

Primulas, not candelabra, but bog adaptable: *P. denticulata* (drumstick primrose), Himalayas. Flower heads are soft lavender globes on upright stems that appear as leaves emerge in earliest spring. Size: 8"–10" tall, 12" spread. Zones (3) 4–7 (8). *P. sieboldii* (siebold primrose), Japan. Purple, white, or rose flowers in clusters of 6–12 in late spring. White form highly recommended. Can grow in more sun and with a little less moisture than other species. Size: 6"–12" tall, 12" spread. Zones (4) 5–8.

RHODODENDRON
Rhododendron
Ericaceae

One low, evergreen azalea species and one tall, deciduous azalea cultivar are grouped here. Soil: acid, moist, well drained, high organic. Partial shade. For detailed information, see "Other Noteworthy Azaleas and Rhododendrons" (page 77).

Rhododendron x *mortieri*

R. kiusianum (kiusianum azalea), Japan. Purple funnel-form flowers cover this small evergreen shrub in mid- to late spring. (Species sometimes pink or white.) Size: 2' tall, equal spread. Zones 6–8 (9). *R. x mortieri* (mortieri azalea), parents from the U.S. (hybrid of native deciduous azaleas). Coral funnel-form flowers in mid- to late spring. Exceptional color. Size: 6' tall, 5' spread. Zones 5–8.

PEONY GARDEN
May

Peonies (*Paeonia* hybrids and species) are one of nature's great gifts to lovers of beauty and especially to the home gardener. Their huge blossoms—singles, doubles, anemone types, and others—come in delectable colors that range from whites and pinks to yellows and glowing reds. Many have handsome yellow

Herbaceous peonies in a range of pinks surround a white decorative beehive. Coral Bells azaleas form the backdrop.

"bosses" of stamens. Ease of culture, hardiness, and longevity add to the appeal of these plants, as does the handsome green foliage that lasts all summer.

In his Peony Garden, H. F. du Pont honored the work of Dr. Percy A. Saunders, one of the great peony hybridizers of the twentieth century. In addition to herbaceous peonies, the garden features the lesser-known tree peony, also easy to grow. These peonies have woody stems that do not die down in winter, yet the term *tree* is misleading since they are actually shrubs that grow four to six feet tall. With petals of tissue-paper delicacy, often frilled and ruffled at the edges, blossoms may measure as much as eight inches across and are among the most sensational exhibits in plantdom. Colors are varied, muted, and unusual, ranging from elegant whites, buffs, pinks, peaches, and yellows to crimson, cerise, and deep maroon. One blossom may contain a combination of hues.

To his Peony Garden, du Pont added plants with similar bloom times, the masterstroke being the introduction of the beauty bush *(Kolkwitzia amabilis)*, with its fountain of cascading pink blossoms. Chinese lilac

Tree peonies, such as Peonia 'Kintagio', *have woody stems and need no staking to keep blossoms upright.*

GARDEN STRUCTURES AND SEATING

What would the Peony Garden be without the Latimeria Summer House or beehives? H. F. du Pont collected many objects for his garden and had structures made for it as well. Such artifacts put a special stamp on a garden, give it distinction, make it memorable. They also become an important part of the design.

You might consider adding an object or artifact to your own garden, in keeping with its mood and that of your home. Sundials, birdbaths, and statuary are easy to come by, as are weathervanes, lanterns, and trellises. Unusual containers (such as a wheelbarrow planted with annuals) can look right at home. Fences and gates offer more possibilities. A bench or chairs are inviting, and furniture for children can add a charming note.

(*Syringa* x *chinensis*) and Henry's lilac (*S.* x *henryi*) also work well here.

Surrounding the garden are more complementary plants. Pink *Weigela florida* var. *venusta*, blooming near the garden steps, harmonizes with the striking wine red *Rhododendron obtusum* 'Amoenum.' A pink crabapple named in honor of du Pont (*Malus* 'Henry F. du Pont') flourishes along the path from the garden to the Visitor Center. The path is lined with Kurume azalea Coral Bells (*Rhododendron* 'Coral Bells').

Three ground covers, all with white flowers, also bloom at this time. Deliciously fragrant lilies of the valley (*Convallaria majalis*), dependable evergreen Japanese pachysandra (*P. terminalis*), and hardy mayapple (*Podophyllum peltatum*), with umbrella-like foliage sheltering its blossoms, flourish here.

Pink Wiegela florida *var.* venusta *and wine red* Rhododendron obtusum *'Ameonum,' shown with mayapple and pachysandra ground covers.*

PLANT SPECIFICS

In the Home Garden

It is usually easy to find a place for a few peonies. They will settle comfortably into a perennial bed or, if placed in a shrub border, will make low, filler material for taller shrubs. The lustrous, dark green foliage of herbaceous peonies is an asset, arriving early and lasting all summer. Fortunately deer and rabbits bother neither herbaceous nor tree peonies. Long-lived plants, they last for decades. In northern climates, they are much prized for their cold hardiness. For southerly situations, early-blooming varieties are recommended.

Tree peonies feature medium green, matte foliage. Their huge blossoms need no staking, so the plant often resembles a big bouquet. Once established, tree peonies do not like to be moved; by contrast, herbaceous peonies can be divided. Both types provide wonderful cut flowers.

Convallaria majalis

CONVALLARIA MAJALIS
Lily of the Valley
Liliaceae
N. America, Europe, Asia
Herbaceous perennial ground cover. Broad-blade leaves. Upright stems bear white, bell-like flowers in midspring; delicious fragrance. Very cold hardy. Propagation: division. Size: 8"–12" tall, equal spread. Soil: good garden. Partial shade to sun. Zones 2–6 (7–8).

Kolkwitzia amabilis

KOLKWITZIA AMABILIS
Beauty Bush
Caprifoliaceae
China
Upright, deciduous shrub. Arching branches. Clusters of pink, flaring, tubular flowers in late spring. Prune after flowering. Propagation: softwood cuttings. Size: 6'–10' tall, 4'–8' spread. Soil: well drained, pH adaptable. Sun. Zones 4–8.

Malus 'Henry F. du Pont'

MALUS 'HENRY F. DU PONT'
Henry F. du Pont Crabapple
Rosaceae
Low-spreading, deciduous tree. Single and semidouble pink flowers in midspring. Prune immediately after flowering. Propagation: softwood cuttings. Size: 20'–30' tall, 25'–35' spread. Soil: acid, moist, well drained. Sun. Zones 4–7.

PACHYSANDRA TERMINALIS
Japanese Pachysandra
Buxaceae
Japan
Evergreen ground cover. Lustrous foliage appears as whorls. Creamy, fragrant, bottle-brush flowers in spring. Spreads fairly aggressively. Foliage handy for flower arrangements. Propagation: division or terminal cuttings in summer. Cultivars available, some variegated. Size: 9"–12" tall, 18" spread. Soil: adaptable. Partial shade. Zones 4–9.

PAEONIA HYBRIDS AND SPECIES
Peony Hybrids and Species
Paeoniaceae
Parents: largely Asian and European
Colors and forms described above. Almost unlimited choices in catalogues. Trouble free, very long-lived. A few that have done well at Winterthur include 'Janice,' in salmon pink that turns to palest pink (herbaceous); 'Ludovica,' deep pink, 'Roman Gold,' large yellow, and 'Chinese Dragon,' deep red (tree peonies).

Paeonia 'Ludovica'

Herbaceous peonies: Plant in fall, with eyes (buds) 2" below soil surface in cold climates, 1" below in warm climates. Once well established, propagate in fall by dividing roots, leaving 3 eyes on each section. Size: 2'–3' tall, equal spread. Soil: moist, well drained, fertile, slightly acid. Sun, but will do well in partial shade. Zones 2–8, with some qualifications at the extremes.

Tree Peonies: Need three weeks of temperatures 35–40°F or below to undergo dormancy. Mostly offered grafted onto herbaceous roots. Plant in fall, with graft union 3"–4" below surface. Prune in February after bud set. Propagation: cuttings taken in September. Size: 4'–8' tall, equal spread. Soil: well drained, fertile, neutral. Partial shade, especially in South. Zones 4–7.

Podophyllum peltatum

PODOPHYLLUM PELTATUM
Mayapple
Berberidaceae
Eastern U.S. and Canada
Herbaceous perennial. Umbrella-like leaves over white, nodding flowers in May. The "apple" looks like a small lemon and comes later. Foliage lasts until fall. Easy. Propagation: division of rhizomes; wear gloves to avoid irritation. Size: 12"–18" tall, 2'–3' spread. Soil: adaptable, will withstand drought. Partial shade. Zones 3–8.

RHODODENDRON
Rhododendron
Ericaceae
Two azaleas are grouped here. For detailed information, see "Other Noteworthy Azaleas and Rhododendrons" (page 77). Soil: acid, moist, well drained, high organic. Partial shade. *R. obtusum* '**Amoenum**' (Amoenum azalea), Japan. Spreading, evergreen azalea; deep wine red flowers in May. Size: 3' tall, equal spread. Zones 6–8 (9). *R.* '**Coral Bells**' (Coral Bells Kurume azalea), Japan. Evergreen azalea; salmon pink hose-in-hose flowers in May. Size: 3' tall, 4' spread. Zones 6–8 (9).

SYRINGA
Lilac
Oleaceae
Two lilacs are found here; one blooms in early May, the other in late May. Both deciduous. Prune soon after flowering by cutting old canes close to ground. Propagation: softwood cuttings. Soil: neutral, pH adaptable, well drained. Sun.

S. x chinensis (Chinese lilac or Rouen lilac), arching branches with lavender flowers early in May. Delicate in appearance.

Syringa chinensis

Size: 8'–15' tall, equal spread. Zones 3–7. *S. x henryi* (Henry's lilac), large, spreading shrub; lavender flowers in late May. Valuable as a late bloomer. Cold hardy. Size: 10' tall, equal spread. Zones 2–7 (8).

WEIGELA FLORIDA
VAR. VENUSTA
Old-Fashioned Weigela
Caprifoliaceae
Deciduous, spreading shrub. Tubelike flowers in small clusters. Purplish pink. Variety *venusta* is more compact than the species. Many cultivars of the species. Early May bloom. Trouble free. Prune after flowering. Propagation: softwood cuttings. Size: 6' tall, equal spread. Soil: any good, not dry. Sun to partial shade. Zones 4–8 (9).

SYCAMORE HILL
Late May–July

As May gives way to June, Winterthur's Sycamore Hill beguiles us with luxuriant blooms in lavender, white, cream, and shades of pink. Trees and shrubs grouped here offer delightful color combinations and suggest many plants for our early-summer gardens.

Named for a 200-year-old sycamore, this area features plants selected to continue the bloom of the surrounding landscape. Fountains of late-blooming lavender lilacs (*Syringa* species and a hybrid), white deutzia (*Deutzia* species and a hybrid), white mock orange (*Philadelphus* cultivars), and the architecturally beautiful white kousa dogwoods (*Cornus kousa*) produce overlapping waves of color and textural interest. Nearby lavender azaleas (*Rhododendron* cultivars) and buddleia

Lavender lilacs and pink Rhododendron *'Homebush' begin the early-summer bloom on Winterthur's Sycamore Hill.*

97

(Buddleia alternifolia) repeat the color of the lilacs, while wine red weigela (*Weigela* 'Eva Rathke') and coral and pink azaleas (*Rhododendron* 'Homebush' and 'Pallas') add contrasting notes.

At the Bristol Summer House, dusty pink blossoms of mountain laurel *(Kalmia latifolia)* echo pink old-fashioned roses (*Rosa* 'Pink Leda'). Later in June, deep pink spirea *(S. x margaritae)* makes an exciting combination with lavender-tinted *Deutzia chunii* and lavender leptodermis. Blending well with all are the creamy blossoms of American fringe trees *(Chionanthus virginicus)* and Japanese tree lilacs *(S. reticulata)*. Later in summer, stewartias (*Stewartia* species) bloom in white.

Rosa *'Pink Leda' flourishes near Winterthur's Bristol Summer House.*

Misty Deutzia chunii (background) *and* Leptodermis oblonga (foreground) *are an inspired pairing.*

PLANT SPECIFICS

In the Home Garden

Several trees stand out as especially valuable. The kousa dogwood, which du Pont sometimes called the June dogwood, has great arching branches covered with star-shape blossoms that look like a coating of white frosting.

A second period of interest comes during the fall berry season, when the trees are laden with raspberry-like fruit. The kousas are easy to grow and bloom later than American dogwoods (C. florida). New hybrids of the two are finding their way into the marketplace and offer further sets of characteristics. Other valuable trees for the home property include American fringe trees, whose creamy blossoms provide the "fringe." The handsome foliage alone makes this tree worth growing, and being native, it is of easy culture. The stewartias are manageable sizes for home grounds and offer appealing architecture, delicate blossoms, unusual fruits, and lovely fall colors.

Buddleia alternifolia

BUDDLEIA ALTERNIFOLIA
Fountain Buddleia
Loganiaceae
China

Deciduous shrub. Arching branches covered with lavender flowers in late spring. Gray-green foliage. Trouble free. Prune after flowering. Propagation: softwood and hardwood cuttings. Size: 6' tall, equal spread. Soil: loose, well drained. Sun. Zones 5–7.

Chionanthus virginicus

CHIONANTHUS VIRGINICUS
American Fringe Tree
Oleaceae
NJ to FL, TX

Deciduous shrub or tree. Handsome foliage. Creamy fringelike flowers in mid May. Prune after flowering. Propagation difficult. Size: 12'–30' tall, equal spread. Soil: acid, moist, well drained, high organic but adaptable. Sun to partial shade. Zones 4–9.

Cornus kousa

CORNUS KOUSA
Kousa Dogwood
Cornaceae
Japan, Korea, China

Deciduous tree. Outstanding in bloom in late spring or early summer, when white bracts coat branches. Trouble free. Many cultivars.

Propagation: softwood cuttings. Size: 20'–30' tall, equal spread. Soil: acid, moist, well drained, organically rich. Sun to light shade. Zones 5–8.

Deutzia x *magnifica*

DEUTZIA
Deutzia
Saxifragaceae

Three deciduous deutzias are grouped here. Prune after flowering. Propagation: softwood or hardwood cuttings. Soil: good garden, pH adaptable, needs moisture. Sun.

    D. chunii (Chunii deutzia), eastern China. Misty lavender in bud, lightens as flowers open. Beautiful, arching shrub; should be better known and grown. Size: 6'–10' tall, equal spread. Zones 5–8.
D. x *magnifica* (showy deutzia), parents from Japan and China. Double, white flowers in short, dense panicles. Arching shrub. Size: 6'–10' tall, equal spread. Zones 5–8.
D. scabra (fuzzy deutzia), Japan, China. Oval shrub; arching branches. White flowers in upright panicles. Cultivars include double flowers. Size: 6'–10' tall, 4'–8' spread. Zones 5–7 (8).

Kalmia latifolia

KALMIA LATIFOLIA
Mountain Laurel
Ericaceae
Eastern U.S.

Evergreen shrub; rather slow growing. Distinctive, pink flowers in round clusters. Handsome, leathery leaves. A favorite native plant. Prune after flowering. Propagation: tissue culture, seed. Many new cultivars, pink through red. Size: 6'–10' tall, equal spread. Soil: acid, cool, moist, well drained. Sun to shade. Zones 4–9.

Leptodermis oblonga

LEPTODERMIS OBLONGA
Chinese Leptodermis
Rubiaceae
Asia

Low, mounded, deciduous shrub. Flowers appear as rosy lavender tubes with open faces in early summer. Prune after flowering. Propagation: seed or softwood cuttings. Size: 3'–4' tall, 4' spread. Soil: good garden. Sun. Zones (4) 5–8.

PHILADELPHUS
Mock Orange
Saxifragaceae

Deciduous shrub. White, fragrant blossoms

Philadelphus x *virginalis* 'Virginal'

in early summer. Easy. Prune after flowering. Propagation: softwood cuttings. Soil: adaptable. Sun to light shade.

Among the many *Philadelphus* growing at Winterthur are **P. x *virginalis* 'Minnesota Snowflake'** (Minnesota Snowflake mock orange), complex parentage. White, double flowers; branches clothed to the ground. Hardy to –30°F. Size: 6'–8' tall, 5'–6' spread. Zones (3) 4–8. **P. x *virginalis* 'Virginal'** (Virginal mock orange), complex parentage. White, semidouble flowers; fragrant. Size: 9' tall, 7' spread. Zones 5–8.

RHODODENDRON
Rhododendron
Ericaceae
Three azaleas, two deciduous and one

Rhododendron 'Martha Hitchcock'

evergreen, are grouped here. Soil: acid, moist, well drained, organic. Partial shade. For detailed information, see "Other Noteworthy Azaleas and Rhododendrons" (page 77).

R. 'Homebush' (Homebush azalea), complex parentage (Knap Hill hybrid). Deciduous. Bright pink, semidouble flowers in late spring. Size: 6'–8' tall, equal spread. Zones 5–8. **R. 'Martha Hitchcock'** (Martha Hitchcock azalea), parents from Asia. Evergreen. White flowers with lavender edge in late spring. A Glenn Dale azalea; bred for large flowers and hardiness in the Mid-Atlantic. Size: 4' tall, equal spread. Zones 6–9. **R. 'Pallas'** (Pallas azalea), complex parentage (Ghent hybrid). Deciduous. Coral, funnel-form flowers in late spring. Size: 6'–10' tall, equal spread. Zones 5–8.

Rosa 'Bess Lovett'

ROSA
Rose
Rosaceae
Extensive hybridization and seedling selection have resulted in complex heritage. Grouped here are two dependable cultivars. Prune in early spring. Propagation: softwood cuttings. Soil: well drained, high organic content. Sun.

R. 'Bess Lovett' (Bess Lovett rose), Wichuraiana hybrid. Deep pink, single blossoms. Disease resistant. Size: 5'–10' tall (climber). Zones (3) 4–8. **R. 'Pink Leda'** (Pink Leda rose), Damask hybrid. Double, pink blossoms in June. Compact. Size: 3' tall, equal spread. Zones 4–9.

Spiraea x margueritae

SPIRAEA x MARGARITAE
Margarita Spirea
Rosaceae
Parents: Asia and U.S.
Deciduous, mounded shrub. Clusters of deep pink flowers in early summer. Trouble free. Prune after flowering. Propagation: softwood or hardwood cuttings. Size: 4' tall, equal spread. Soil: any good garden. Sun. Zones 4–8.

Stewartia pseudocamellia or *S. koreana*

STEWARTIA
Stewartia
Theaceae
Beautiful flowers, foliage, and habit distinguish stewartias. Three modest-size deciduous trees are grouped here (although some taxonomists believe that *S. koreana* and *S. pseudocamellia* are the same). Trouble free. Soil: acid, moist, well drained, organically rich.

   S. koreana (Korean stewartia), Korea. White, cup-shape flowers in early summer. Beautiful round buds, leaves. Exfoliating bark. Excellent fall color. Cultivars available. Little pruning required. Propagation: June cuttings. Size: 20'–30' tall, equal spread.

Sun to partial shade. Zones 5–7. **S. ovata** (mountain stewartia), NC, TN, FL. Small tree or shrub; white, cupped, crepe-paper flowers in summer. Propagation difficult. Size: 10'–15' tall, equal spread. Partial shade. Zones 5–8. **S. pseudocamellia** (Japanese stewartia), Japan. See *S. koreana*. Size: 20'–40' tall, equal spread. Partial shade. Zones (4) 5–7.

SYRINGA
Lilac
Oleaceae
Two shrubs and one tree are grouped here, all deciduous. Prune after flowering. Propagation: softwood cuttings. Soil: neutral, pH adaptable, well drained. Sun.

   S. x henryi (Henry's lilac), parents from China and Hungary. Large, spreading shrub. Lavender flowers. Valuable as a late bloomer. Cold hardy. Size: 10' tall, equal spread. Zones 2–7 (8). **S. meyeri** (Meyer lilac), China. Rounded shrub. Lavender flowers. Excellent bloomer. Modest size. Mildew resistant. Size: 4'–8' tall, 6'–12' spread. Zones 3–7. **S. reticulata** (Japanese tree lilac), Japan. Creamy white flowers appear in June on this small tree. Relatively trouble free. Many cultivars. Size: 20'–30' tall, 15'–25' spread. Zones 3–7.

Weigela 'Eva Rathke,' with lavender *Buddleia alternifolia*

WEIGELA 'EVA RATHKE'
Eva Rathke Weigela
Caprifoliaceae
Parents: Asia
Compact, deciduous shrub. Deep wine red flowers in late May. Trouble free. Prune after flowering. Propagation: softwood cuttings. Size: 5' tall, equal spread. Soil: any good garden; not dry. Sun. Zones 5–8 (9).

Summer

"Summer's lease hath all
too short a date."

— William Shakespeare, Sonnet 18

Summer days are a time to enjoy the outdoors. Yards and gardens
become extensions of our houses, as porches, patios, and pools
become centers of activity — or contented loafing. Two gardens with
water, described here, may hold ideas for you. The Reflecting Pool
is formal, architectural, and sun drenched; the Glade Garden
is naturalistic and shady. Rounding out the chapter is a fine collection
of summer-blooming shrubs and trees, all able to add vitality
to a summer garden.

*Opener and left: Winterthur's Glade Garden offers a cool,
sheltered retreat on warm days. A canopy of trees, a waterfall,
pools, and lush greenery contribute to a feeling of serenity.*

GLADE GARDEN
June–July

Glade: the term conjures up a shady retreat, and the Glade Garden indeed offers a peaceful and refreshing respite from summer heat. This garden provides several easy-to-grow plants that would enhance tree-sheltered water features on your property.

The Glade Garden features a babbling waterfall that flows into a pool, where bright orange koi glide beneath the surface. Clumps of slender iris mark the edge of the water, and reflected on its surface are the large trees overhead and the colorful plants beside it. This pool empties into a second, lower one; the two are separated by a walkway that allows close viewing of the fish and perhaps a glimpse of the bullfrog whose deep croak occasionally startles the casual visitor.

Brightly colored koi swim amidst reflections of orange daylilies (Hemerocallis fulva).

Hydrangeas (hortensia, right, and lace-cap, left) bloom with daylilies and ferns on the walkway between the pools.

In early summer, creamy white lace-cap and mophead hydrangeas (*Hydrangea arborescens* and *H. arborescens* 'Grandiflora') and graceful orange daylilies (*Hemerocallis fulva*) bloom around the pools. Rich purple hostas (*Hosta ventricosa*) and lavender roving bellflowers (*Campanula rapunculoides*) also thrive here.

In the Home Garden

Hostas are well known to most gardeners as practical ground covers for shady places. Although competing with many on the market, Hosta ventricosa *has a robust purple color to commend it. It works well here, being of intensity similar to the orange and cream of accompanying plants. Numerous new daylilies are also on the market, but the old favorite orange daylily, tall and graceful, retains a place in naturalistic and woodland gardens. If cut to the ground after blooming (a Winterthur practice), new foliage will quickly emerge and last until late fall. Roving bellflower spreads quickly and is suitable for naturalized areas of considerable size.*

Campanula rapunculoides

Hemerocallis fulva

CAMPANULA RAPUNCULOIDES

Roving Bellflower
Campanulaceae
Europe

Herbaceous perennial. Nodding, lavender, funnel-form flowers on erect stems. Summer bloom. Spreads by seeding and underground runners; may become invasive. Good for naturalized areas. Size: 2'–4' tall, 2' spread. Soil: neutral, adaptable. Sun to partial shade. Zones 3–5 (6).

HEMEROCALLIS FULVA

Orange Daylily
Liliaceae
Europe and Asia

Herbaceous perennial; common orange daylily now naturalized in the eastern U.S. Bladelike leaves. Trumpet-shape flowers. Of easy culture. Propagation: division. Size: 2'–3' tall, equal spread. Soil: adaptable. Sun to partial shade. Zones (2) 3–9.

Hosta ventricosa

H. arborescens 'Grandiflora'

HOSTA VENTRICOSA
Blue Hosta
Liliaceae
Japan, Siberia
Herbaceous plant; forms clumps of handsome, large leaves. In midsummer, rich purple flowers open on tall spikes. Propagation: division in early spring. Size: 3' tall, equal spread. Soil: moist, well drained, high organic content. Shade to partial shade. Zones 3–9.

HYDRANGEA ARBORESCENS
Smooth Hydrangea
Hydrangeaceae
NY to FL
Deciduous, mounding shrub. Clusters of flowers turn from green to creamy white in summer. Hydrangeas are divided into lacecap types (ring of large, sterile flowers surrounding a center of smaller fertile flowers); and hortensias, or mopheads (large, sterile flowers that form a ball). Many cultivars of both types available. Trouble free. Grows well at the shore. Often dried for flower arrangements. Prune in spring. Propagation: softwood cuttings.

H. arborescens '**Grandiflora**' (Hills of Snow hydrangea), rounded clusters of large, sterile flowers. This and other variations were found in the wild and cultivated. Size: 3'–5' tall, equal spread. Soil: pH adaptable; likes rich, moist, well drained. Partial shade to shade; sun, if sufficient moisture is available. Zones 3–9.

Iris pseudacorus

IRIS PSEUDACORUS
Yellow Flag
Iridaceae
Europe; naturalized in eastern U.S.
Herbaceous plant. Bladelike leaves; elegant buds. Flowers with yellow falls and lighter standards in late spring. Grows in water, bogs, or drier situations if additional water is provided. Propagation: division. Many cultivars. Size: 2'–3' tall, 2' spread. Soil: moist, acid, organically rich. Sun or partial shade. Zones 5–9.

WATER IN YOUR GARDEN

Water is a superb garden feature. The sounds of water, its cooling effects, attractiveness to birds, and surface reflections add much to our enjoyment. If your property lacks water features, you might consider some of the commercially available devices and supplies that enable home gardeners to create them. You may choose from a wide variety of pools, pumps, aquatic plants, fish, and much more to add a new dimension to your landscape. If space is limited, a simple barrel-and-pump arrangement will add many of the attributes of water and attract birds to your garden as well.

With the fullness of foliage in summer, a few bright accents suffice.

REFLECTING POOL AND CONTAINER PLANTS
May–October

The architecture of the Reflecting Pool area, of Italian Renaissance influence, is a joy at all seasons. Superbly proportioned stairways, walls, and archways—beautiful in their own right—afford a marvelous setting for the plants that grow here. A well-planned palette of plant material, with something almost always in bloom, gives changing prospects throughout the year and provides inspiration for our own gardens.

In the springtime, favorite azaleas and dogwoods are lush and colorful in pink, white, and lavender. Tree peonies flower in pale pink, while a delightful vine, soft pink *Clematis montana* var. *rubens*, clambers over an ironwork arch. In the summer, when the mirrorlike pool and the sounds of fountains are refreshing, this area takes on an entirely new look. Bright annuals and perennials fill decorative containers, and exotic lotuses (*Nelumbo* species and cultivars) and water lilies (*Nymphaea* cultivars) flourish in the pool.

In August and September, two permanent herbaceous plants bloom here. Hardy begonia *(Begonia grandis)* nestles into corners of gray stonework—a super background for its pink pouchlike buds, flat blossoms, and handsome foliage. And growing in large numbers is that most practical of ground covers, lily-turf (*Liriope muscari*), with purple gumdrop-like blossoms.

CONTAINER PLANTS

Growing plants in decorative containers is a field in itself. The practice becomes more popular each year

Pansies in bowls grow under a flowering dogwood.

Nierembergia *'Mont Blanc'* (foreground), *white geranium, and striated leaves of* Chlorophytum commosum *'Variegatum'* *handsomely fill a bowl beside the Reflecting Pool.*

as homeowners embellish decks, patios, and entrance-ways with potted plants and even incorporate them—pots and all—into the garden.

Container plantings can completely change the look of a garden from year to year, season to season, even month to month. Those around Winterthur's Reflecting Pool vary each year. In the past the area has been enhanced with such favorites as shocking pink geraniums, lavender ageratum, silver dusty miller, pink pentas, and sky blue agapanthus. Du Pont sometimes lined the staircases with fuchsias, their earring-drop blossoms seeming perfect for the purpose. A recent color scheme included red 'Dragon Wing' begonias, while white *Nierembergia* 'Mont Blanc' and white geraniums (*Pelargonium* cultivar) grew with spider plant (*Chlorophytum commosum* 'Variegatum') in bowls around the pool. On the staircase were a white mandevilla (*Mandevilla* x *amabilis* 'Monte'), red fuchsias (*Fuchsia magellanica* 'Versicolor'), and nearby a white oleander (*Nerium oleander*).

White Mandevilla *x* amabilis *'Monte' graces the stair landing, flanked by red* Fuchsia magellanica *'Versicolor.'*

In the Home Garden

There seems to be a trend toward using plants in containers in the garden proper, especially in a perennial bed. This practice offers an easy solution to certain design problems, for a pot can provide a splash of instant color just where needed. When conditions change later in the season, the pot can be moved, filled with something else, or simply stowed away as the bed fills up.

If you have a place for a vine, consider pink anemone clematis, a spring-blooming favorite for clambering over a fence or trellis. Another possibility is mandevilla, increasingly popular as a summer-blooming potted plant and now available in many colors.

A pool is not necessary to grow small lotuses or water lilies; these can be cultivated in simple tubs or barrels. A tub that measures two feet across is adequate for small aquatic plants and would be a fun way to try out water gardening.

Begonia grandis

BEGONIA
Begonia
Begoniaceae

Herbaceous plant; many forms. Grown for beautiful flowers/leaves. **B. hybrid 'Dragon Wing'** (red Dragon Wing begonia), complex parentage. Red or pink flowers available in the Dragon Wing series, similar to angel-wing begonias from Brazil. Glossy green leaves, somewhat pendulous flowers in clusters. Constant bloom, self-cleaning, heat tolerant. Propagation: cuttings, seed. Size: 12" tall, 18" spread. Soil: moist, well drained, organically rich. Sun to partial shade. Zone 10 (tender perennial). **B. grandis** (hardy begonia), Asia. Large, green, heart-shape leaves. Soft pink, pouchlike buds; flat flowers in late summer. Propagation: bulblets, seed. Size: 2'–3' tall, equal spread. Soil: moist, well drained, organically rich. Partial shade to shade. Zones 6–9.

CENTAUREA GYMNOCARPA 'COLCHESTER WHITE'
Dusty Miller
Asteraceae
Capri

One of many plants called dusty miller, this one is large, handsome, and has arching branches

Centaurea gymnocarpa 'Colchester White,' white *Nierembergia* 'Mont Blanc,' and *Coleus* x *hybridus* 'Wizard Velvet'

with gray to whitish dissected leaves and lavender flowers. Trouble free. Propagation: cuttings, seed. Size: 2' tall, equal spread. Soil: good garden. Sun. Zones 8–10 (tender perennial).

CHLOROPHYTUM COMMOSUM 'VARIEGATUM'
Spider Plant
Liliaceae
S. Africa

Long, slender blades of striated foliage, green and cream. Plantlets on long stalks allow for easy propagation. Size: 3' tall, 2' spread. Soil: moist, well drained. Sun or shade. Zone 10 (tender perennial).

CLEMATIS MONTANA VAR. RUBENS
Pink Anemone Clematis
Ranunculaceae
China

Deciduous vine. Soft pink flowers in spring. Prune after flowering. Propagation: softwood

Clematis montana var. *rubens*

cuttings. Size: 20' tall. Soil: fertile, well drained. Sun, shade for roots. Zones 5–8.

COLEUS x HYBRIDUS 'WIZARD VELVET'
Velvet Coleus
Lamiaceae
Complex parentage
Red-foliage plant. Color varies with light conditions. Propagation: cuttings; will root in water. Size: 1'–2' tall, equal spread. Soil: good garden. Sun to partial shade. Zone 10 (tender perennial).

FUCHSIA MAGELLANICA 'VERSICOLOR'
Versicolor Fuchsia
Onagraceae
Species: Peru, Chile
Hanging red and purple flowers in summer. Propagation: tip cuttings. Size: 1'–3' tall, equal spread. Soil: moist, well drained, fertile. Sun to partial shade. Zones 8–10 (tender perennial).

HEDERA HELIX
English Ivy
Araliaceae
Species: Europe

Evergreen vine, grown for foliage, indoors and out. Many wonderful cultivars. Propagation: cuttings; will root in water. Soil: good garden. Partial shade. Zones 5–8.

IMPATIENS WALLERIANA HYBRID
Impatiens
Balsaminaceae
Species: Africa
Herbaceous perennial. Popular bedding and container plant good for shady areas. Many colors as well as white available. Blooms continuously, summer through fall. Needs no deadheading. Easy, dependable. Propagation: cuttings. Size: 1'–2' tall, 2' spread. Soil: good garden. Shade to partial shade. Zones 10–11 (tender perennial).

LIRIOPE MUSCARI
Blue Lily-Turf
Liliaceae
Asia
Practical ground cover with clumps of strap-like, evergreen foliage. Lavender flowers on upright stalks in late summer. Withstands heat, drought. Few diseases or pests. Cut back in spring. Propagation: division, seeds.

Liriope muscari

Many cultivars. Size: 12"–18" tall, 12" spread. Soil: adaptable. Sun to shade. Zones 6–9.

Mandevilla x *amabilis* 'Monte'

MANDEVILLA x AMABILIS 'MONTE'
Monte Mandevilla
Apocynaceae
Complex parentage
Woody, twining vine. Glossy foliage. Flat, white flowers in summer. Propagation: softwood cuttings. Size: 10'–12' tall. Soil: moist, well drained, high organic. Sun. Zones 10–11 (tender perennial).

NELUMBO
Lotus
Nelumbonaceae
Handsome aquatic plants. Large, saucer-shape leaves and multipetaled, cupped blossoms. Distinctive seed pods. Hardy if roots are below frost line. Propagation: division of tubers in spring. Size: 3'–7' tall, 3' spread. Plant in containers in heavy, neutral soil topped with sand or gravel, then sink. Sun. Zones 4–11.

Noteworthy species and cultivars include: *N. lutea* (American lotus), Ontario to TX. Pale yellow flowers. Easy to grow.

Nelumbo 'Speciosum Pink'

N. nucifera (East Indian lotus), Asia to Australia. Pink or white flowers. *N.* **'Mrs. Perry D. Slocum,'** pink flowers that change to yellow. *N.* **'Roseum plenum,'** pink flowers. Other cultivars of varying sizes.

NERIUM OLEANDER
Oleander
Apocynaceae
Mediterranean region
Tender evergreen perennial; often grown as a greenhouse plant. Clusters of white, pink, red, or purple phloxlike flowers.

Nerium oleander

Summer blooming; withstands drought. Cut back after flowering. Leaves and sap toxic. Propagation: cuttings, seeds. Many cultivars. Size: 5'–20' tall. Soil: well drained, organic. Sun to partial shade. Zones 8–11.

NIEREMBERGIA 'MONT BLANC'
White Cupflower
Solanaceae
Species: S. America
Tender herbaceous perennial. Open-faced, white flowers and attractive foliage. Size:

4"–6" tall, 10" spread. Soil: good container or garden. Sun. Zones 7–10.

Nymphaea 'Odorata Gigantea'

NYMPHAEA CULTIVARS
Water Lilies
Nymphaeaceae
Complex parentage
Hardy cultivars: round leaves and lilylike flowers that float on water surface. Tender cultivars: leaves and flowers rise above the surface. **'Charlene Strawn'** (yellow) and **'Pink Opal'** are good hardy cultivars. Many cultivars, including red, yellow, pink, salmon, and white. Plant in containers in heavy, neutral soil topped with sand or gravel, then sink. Sun. Zones depend on cultivar.

STONEWORK

Splendid architectural elements remind us that what is built in stone is enduring, requires little care, and can be very beautiful. Although the Italianate style is quite grand, more informal effects can be achieved in the home landscape through the use of retaining walls, stone walkways, or steps. Such features bring lasting pleasure and are a wonderful foil for plants. The homeowner, with a good how-to book, can undertake modest stone projects (see "Suggested Reading," page 172).

PLANTS FOR SUMMER BLOOM
July–September

What brightens our gardens when the great bounty of spring bloom subsides? Certainly there is the lexicon of summer annuals. But what of woody plants and complementary herbaceous perennials that bloom in summer? Fortunately there are some late bloomers among the shrubs and trees, many with the desirable trait of a long bloom time. For this reason and because these plants are relatively few in number, each one is noteworthy, offering a lift to summer gardens.

PATIO GARDEN

From summer into fall, the Patio Garden beside the Reflecting Pool at Winterthur showcases pink, lavender,

Natchez crape-myrtle anchors corners of Winterthur's Patio Garden, where it grows beside a hedge of Diana hibiscus.

and white flowers. Outstanding among the shrubs is Diana hibiscus (*Hibiscus syriacus* 'Diana'), which covers itself with large, single, white blossoms from July through September. Five-petaled blooms, some cupped, some flat, appear against dark green leaves and are cooling on hot late-summer days. Fading blooms seem miraculously to take care of themselves. White crape-myrtle (*Lagerstroemia* 'Natchez') grows companionably on each side of the hibiscus.

In August, summer sweet clethra (*Clethra alnifolia*) produces fragrant white spires and is followed by fragrant white hosta (*Hosta* 'Royal Standard'). In September, *Hydrangea paniculata* 'Tardiva' opens white panicles that gradually turn rosy pink, a color that is picked up by the glossy abelia (*Abelia* x *grandiflora*), which produces soft pink flowers and long-lasting rosy sepals from July until frost. Under all, lavender rose astilbe (*Astilbe chinensis* var. *pumila*) blooms for many weeks.

From July through September, misty lavender Russian sage (Perovskia atriplicifolia) creates a captivating vista at Winterthur's Magnolia Bend.

MAGNOLIA BEND IN LATE SUMMER

From July through September, feathery spires of Russian sage *(Perovskia atriplicifolia)* form a lavender mist against the deep greens of Magnolia Bend. Tiny lavender flowers are spaced out along tapered stems, and small, gray-green leaves add to the plant's delicate airiness. Perovskia may be combined with other woody plants, as it is here, or placed in a herbaceous border, where it would also be in scale. Some writers classify perovskia as a herbaceous perennial, but the lower stems actually become quite woody, and it is reliably permanent where hardy. Butterflies like it, and when dried, it gives off a pleasant sagelike aroma. In late August, it is joined by a lavender aster *(Aster spectabilis)* for a marriage made in heaven. Complementing all is the practical ground cover leadwort *(Ceratostigma plumbaginoides)*, whose bright blue flowers, touches of maroon, and green leaves produce a nicely blending hue. This simple combination of shades of lavender and green is remarkably effective for weeks in late summer.

SUMMER-BLOOMING TREES

Yellowwood *(Cladrastis kentukea)* is a handsome native tree that seems underused but would be a fine addition to almost any lawn. Rounded in form with lively green foliage, in June this tree has pendulous, white, fragrant blossoms. Another native of fine form is the franklinia *(Franklinia alatamaha)*, or Franklin tree, which grows on the edge of a stream by the Old Main Drive. In July this tree bears exquisite, white, cupped flowers with orange centers. Graceful foliage turns red, purple, and gold in the fall.

Crape-myrtle softens architectural lines at East Circle.

Also in July, goldenrain trees *(Koelreuteria paniculata)* flower in attractive, yellow, upright sprays. Looking more like sunshine than rain, the blossoms are followed by light greenish seedpods that last a long time and may be responsible for its common name. The color of the seedpods relates nicely to the creamy blossoms of sophora *(Sophora japonica)*, or Japanese pagoda tree, that appear nearby. With a rounded crown at maturity, the sophora is noted for giving the soft, dappled shade often desired near a house; it also tolerates urban conditions.

SUMMER-BLOOMING SHRUBS

Blue, lavender, pink, rose, and white are all represented in the many summer-blooming hydrangea cultivars. Of special note are Preziosa *(H. serrata* 'Preziosa'), a soft lavender hortensia (ball type) that turns pink and then deep mauvy rose, and the lovely pink and blue lace-caps, such as Blue Billow *(H. macrophylla*

'Blue Billow'). These are just two of the numerous hydrangea introductions on today's market.

Other July-blooming shrubs that make nice additions to the home garden are chaste-trees (*Vitex agnus-castus* species and cultivars), in lavender, pink, and white, as well as *Hibiscus syriacus* 'Bluebird,' found near the Visitor Parking Area at Winterthur. Panicle hydrangeas *(Hydrangea paniculata)* bloom later, producing huge, white, cone-shape inflorescences that gradually turn rosy and blend well with a clear pink crape-myrtle (*Lagerstroemia indica* 'Potomac').

On Oak Hill, caryopteris (*Caryopteris* x *clandonensis* 'Longwood Blue'), also called bluebeard, blooms from August through September. This low-growing shrub has violet blue flowers that bloom from the lower fascicles to the upper ones, for a long season of flower. It is attractive to butterflies and bothered by few pests or diseases. In addition, caryopteris provides excellent cut-flower material since it is easy to "make stay" where you place it and lasts well in water. The flowers combine well with yellow, and its grayish green foliage is a fine foil for many other colors.

Preziosa hydrangea turns from lavender to pink, and then deep mauvy rose. Here it grows beside blue and pink lace-cap hydrangeas.

In the Home Garden

Almost all of these plants are "easy," meaning that they are adaptable and relatively problem free. Ease of culture is certainly appealing as the days grow warmer and sitting by our gardens is more enticing than working in them. These dependable plants include such shrubs as perovskia, abelia, clethra, caryopteris, hibiscus, and hydrangeas. For low-growing ground covers, consider dwarf Chinese astilbe, leadwort, and hostas. As for trees, sophora, koelreuteria, and yellowwood all seem to be trouble free.

Yet there are more delicate plants that by virtue of their beauty inspire us to plant and nurture them. One of these is franklinia. In addition to delicate blossoms, graceful foliage, good habit, and notable fall color, this tree is an excellent size for the home property. If you are inspired, it is worthy of the best efforts.

Abelia x *grandiflora*

ABELIA X GRANDIFLORA
Glossy Abelia
Caprifoliaceae
Parents: China
Semi-evergreen, spreading shrub. White-tinged-pink, funnel-form flowers; long-lasting rosy sepals. Trouble free. Prune in spring. Propagation: softwood cuttings. Cultivars available. Size: 3'–6' tall, equal spread. Soil: acid, moist, well drained. Sun to partial shade. Zones (5) 6–9.

ASTILBE CHINENSIS VAR. PUMILA
Dwarf Chinese Astilbe

Astilbe chinensis var. *pumila*

Saxifragaceae
China
Herbaceous perennial. Fuzzy, lavender rose, upright panicles bloom in midsummer. Propagation: division. Size: 12"–18" tall, equal spread. Soil: moist, well drained, organically rich. Partial shade to shade. Zones 4–8.

Aster spectabilis

ASTER SPECTABILIS
Showy Aster
Asteraceae
MA to NC
Herbaceous perennial. Lavender, daisylike flowers in late summer. Spreads by runners. Propagation: division or terminal cuttings. Size: 1'–2' tall, equal spread. Soil: dry, sandy. Sun. Zones 5–8.

CARYOPTERIS X CLANDONENSIS 'LONGWOOD BLUE'
Longwood Blue Bluebeard
Verbenaceae
Parents: Asia
Deciduous shrub; full, rounded shape. Gray-green foliage. Violet blue flowers in late summer. Easy. Avoid excessive fertilization.

Caryopteris x *clandonensis* 'Longwood Blue'

Cut back in spring. Many other cultivars. Propagation: softwood cuttings. Size: 3'–4' tall, equal spread. Soil: loose, well drained. Sun. Zones 6–9.

Ceratostigma plumbaginoides

CERATOSTIGMA PLUMBAGINOIDES
Leadwort
Plumbaginaceae
China

Herbaceous perennial. Royal blue flowers in late summer and fall. Plant takes on reddish cast in fall. Good for ground cover, containers. Propagation: cuttings or division in spring.

Size: 8"–12" tall, 18" spread. Soil: adaptable. Sun to partial shade. Zones 5–8.

Cladrastis kentukea

CLADRASTIS KENTUKEA
(FORMERLY LUTEA)
American Yellowwood
Fabaceae
Eastern U.S.

Deciduous tree. Rounded crown; graceful, white, pendulous flowers in early summer. Trouble free. Prune only in summer to avoid bleeding. Propagation: December cuttings. Size: 30'–50' tall, 40'–55' spread. Soil: adaptable, well drained. Sun. Zones 4–8.

CLETHRA ALNIFOLIA
Summer Sweet Clethra
Clethraceae
Eastern U.S.

Deciduous shrub. Fragrant, white, upright panicles of flowers in late summer. Good yellow fall color. Easy. Cultivars available,

Clethra alnifolia

some pink. Size: 4'–8' tall, equal spread. Soil: moist, acid. Sun to partial shade. Zones 4–8.

Franklinia alatamaha

FRANKLINIA ALATAMAHA
Franklinia
Theaceae
GA

Small deciduous tree. Flowers with white, crepe-paper petals and orange stamens in late summer. Red and purple fall foliage. Propagation: softwood cuttings. Size: 10'–20' tall, 6'–15' spread. Soil: acid, consistently moist, well drained, organically rich. Sun to light shade. Zones 5–8 (9).

Hibiscus syriacus 'Bluebird'

HIBISCUS SYRIACUS
Rose of Sharon
Malvaceae
China, India

Deciduous shrubs. Bloom in summer. Many cultivars, from white to pink, red, lavender, purple. Prune in spring. Propagation: softwood cuttings. Soil: adaptable, but prefers moist, well drained. Sun to partial shade.

H. syriacus **'Bluebird,'** lavender blue. Size: 8'–12' tall, 6'–10' spread. Zones 5–8 (9). *H. syriacus* **'Diana,'** white, a triploid; features five-petaled blooms, some cupped, some flat, against dark green leaves. Long bloom period. Does not set seed, so self-sown seedlings are not a problem. Size: 8'–12' tall, 6'–10' spread. Zones 5–8 (9).

HOSTA 'ROYAL STANDARD'
Royal Standard Hosta
Liliaceae
Parentage complex

Herbaceous plant. Handsome, large leaves form clumps. Fragrant, white, lilylike flowers on tall spikes in late summer. Propagation:

Hosta 'Royal Standard'

division in early spring. Size: 2'–3' tall, equal spread. Soil: rich, well drained, consistently moist. Partial shade to shade. Zones 3–9.

HYDRANGEA
SPECIES AND CULTIVARS
Hydrangeaceae

Hydrangeas described below are deciduous and bloom in summer and early fall. Trouble free. Grow well by the sea. Propagation: softwood cuttings.

H. macrophylla **'Blue Billow'** (Blue Billow hydrangea), Korea. Blue lace-cap type. If necessary, acidify soil with aluminum sulfate since blueness in hydrangeas depends on availability of aluminum ions. Prune after flowering. Size: 3'–6' tall, equal spread. Zones 6–9. Soil: moist, well drained, porous; plant droops if dry. Sun to partial shade. *H. paniculata* (panicle hydrangea), Japan, China. White, then rose, flowers in late summer and early fall. Mixture of showy, sterile flowers and inconspicuous, fertile flowers. Prune in spring. Some cultivars are pink. Size: 10'–20' tall, equal spread. Soil: moist, rich. Sun to partial shade. Zones 3–8. *H. paniculata* **'Grandiflora'** (Pee Gee hydrangea) is a cultivar

with more sterile (conspicuous) flowers in clusters, causing stems to arch. Prune in spring. *H. paniculata* **'Tardiva'** (Tardiva hydrangea) has an attractive mixture of sterile (conspicuous) and fertile (inconspicuous) white flowers. Late blooming. Prune in spring. *H. serrata* **'Preziosa'** (Preziosa hydrangea), Japan, Korea. Lavender hortensia, turns pink then mauve rose. Prune after flowering. Size: 4' tall, equal spread. Soil: moist, well drained, acid or neutral. Sun to partial shade. Zones (5) 6–7.

Koelreuteria paniculata

KOELREUTERIA PANICULATA
Goldenrain Tree
Sapindaceae
China, Japan, Korea

Deciduous, rounded tree. Upright sprays of yellow flowers in midsummer. Showy, light greenish fruits follow. Prune during winter. Propagation: hardwood cuttings. Size: 30'–40' tall, equal spread. Soil: adaptable. Sun. Zones (4) 5–8.

Lagerstroemia at East Circle

LAGERSTROEMIA
Crape-Myrtle
Lythraceae
Trees or shrubs of warm climates. Soil: moist, well drained. Sun. **L. indica** (common crape-myrtle), China, Korea. Upright, deciduous shrub. Summer bloom of cone-shape panicles on arching branches. Species and cultivar colors range from white to pink, purple, red. Cultivars in various heights. Prune in spring or immediately after flowering. Propagation: seed, softwood cuttings. Size: 8'–25' tall, equal spread. Zones (6) 7–9. **L. indica 'Potomac'**

(Potomac crape- myrtle) is pink. Size: 10' tall, 8' spread. Zones (6) 7–9. **L. indica x L. fauriei 'Natchez'** (Natchez crape-myrtle), parents from China and Japan. Deciduous shrub or tree. White flowers in summer. Cinnamon-colored bark. Good fall color. Size: 20' tall, equal spread. Zones (6) 7–9.

PEROVSKIA ATRIPLICIFOLIA
Russian Sage
Lamiaceae
Afghanistan to Tibet
Somewhat woody perennial. Misty, lavender flowers in late summer into fall. Trouble free. Cut back in spring or fall. Propagation: softwood cuttings. Cultivars available. Size: 3'–4' tall, 4' spread. Soil: well drained, adaptable. Sun. Zones 5–9.

SOPHORA JAPONICA
Japanese Pagoda Tree
Leguminosae
China, Korea
Deciduous, round-headed tree. Clusters of hanging, creamy flowers in late summer. Trouble free. Propagation: softwood cuttings.

Sophora japonica

Size: 50'–70' tall, equal spread. Soil: well drained, adaptable. Sun. Zones 4–7.

VITEX AGNUS-CASTUS
Chaste-Tree
Verbenaceae
Europe and Asia
Deciduous shrub; spreading habit. Palmate leaves, panicles of lavender flowers in midsummer. Trouble free. Prune early spring. Propagation: softwood cuttings. Many cultivars, including deeper lavender, pink, and white forms. Size: 8'–10' tall, equal spread. Soil: moist, well drained, neutral. Sun. Zones (6) 7–8 (9).

THE LOST TREE

John Bartram, an early plant hunter from Philadelphia, found the franklinia tree growing in Georgia in 1770. He named it for fellow Philadelphian Benjamin Franklin and subsequently obtained a few plants for his own garden. That was most fortunate, for no other franklinias have been found growing in the wild since 1790. If you own a franklinia, as you probably know, you have a descendant of one of Bartram's original trees.

Vitex agnus-castus

Summer into Fall

"And when you plant your
rose-trees, plant them deep,
having regard to bushes all aflame."

—*Vita Sackville-West,* The Land, *1926*

As fall approaches and nature turns on multicolored effects all around, we look up and out and appreciate anew our views and vistas. What we planted in the spring has an entirely different look at this season, but it is the ever-changing landscape that keeps us enthralled. Since nature is a consummate colorist, our "bushes all aflame" are consistently pleasing together and, in fact, enhance one another. Fall also brings berries in abundance, adding texture and additional color. Wildflowers and fall-flowering bulbs impart ground-level interest. Explore the rich panoply of summer-into-fall enchantment at Winterthur.

Opener: Pond reflections heighten the impact of nature's fall beauty.

Left: Sternbergia lutea

WILDFLOWERS OF SUMMER AND FALL
June–October

Wildflowers continue to be an important part of the Winterthur landscape during summer and fall, enhancing vistas through their naturalistic charm. Given the diverse growing conditions here, you will find plants suitable for a variety of situations on your property.

WATER'S-EDGE PLANTS
Winterthur is endowed with many small springs, streams, and ponds where moisture-loving plants thrive.

Easy to grow and informal, cup plant (Silphium perfoliatum) *needs a large site.*

These sites include the Quarry and Glade Gardens and Clenny Run, which travels the length of the estate and supplies water for the several ponds.

In June, forget-me-nots *(Myosotis scorpioides)* form large flowering clumps that hug the banks of Clenny Run. Although individual flowers are not showy, en masse they make a lovely drift of blue. This type of forget-me-not grows naturally in water, but species *M. sylvatica* and *M. alpestris* have a similar look and are easy to grow in garden soil.

Cup plant *(Silphium perfoliatum)* also grows along Clenny Run, bearing an abundance of bright yellow flowers with dark centers in July. The term *perfoliatum* refers to the leaves, which are joined in pairs around the stem to form cuplike wells, giving the plant its common name. Native to the prairies of the West, among other places, cup plant does not require the constant moisture that the stream provides, but it does need a large site and a rather informal situation. It is easy to grow.

In August, swamp rose mallow *(Hibiscus moscheutos)*, belying its inelegant common name, produces spectacular blossoms in red, pink, and white, reminiscent of holly-hock flowers. Large plants with large blossoms (up to eight inches), they need sun, good air circulation, and consistent moisture.

In October all the streams on the estate are banked with soft lavender swamp aster *(Aster puniceus)*, another plant with an unlovely common name. Although individual blossoms are not significant, in large numbers they make a soft cloud of lavender. This aster is valuable for damp, wetland conditions.

Aster puniceus, *so-called swamp aster, sends up clouds of lavender to outline streams in the fall.*

FLOWERS OF FIELDS AND WOODLANDS

Growing in open meadows is that old favorite, Queen Anne's lace *(Daucus carota)*, whose July-blooming, lacy, white flowers are the delight of flower arrangers. As the plant goes to seed, old flower clusters curl to form an intriguing "bird's nest," which provides another of the plant's common names. Although it looks more like a bird's cage than a nest, children enjoy searching out this distinctive detail. Not recommended for the cultivated garden because of its spreading habit, this plant is a good choice for a wildflower meadow.

In October more flower-arranging material blooms in the form of soft yellow wreath goldenrod *(Solidago caesia)* that grows in the woodlands of the Winterthur estate. Most goldenrod species are tall and feature flowers in a plumelike top. This species, by contrast, has flowers along an arching stem of about two feet and would be pleasing in a garden or for an arrangement indoors.

Also growing in abundance is white snakeroot *(Eupatorium rugosum)*, with fuzzy, white flowers in flat-topped clusters, similar to annual ageratum. A more attractive common name would be nice, but the plant is full and floriferous in October, when it lends charm to many areas of the estate. The flowers last a long time in both the garden and arrangements.

White wood aster *(Aster divaricatus)* is among the great genus of asters that are such important fall plants. Cheerful and carefree, this species is quite undemanding and grows in a number of situations. Its few ray flowers (petals) give it the appearance of an asterisk or a star.

A garden path lined with yellow wreath goldenrod (Solidago caesia), *white snakeroot* (Eupatorium rugosum), *and white wood aster. Foliage of oak-leaf hydrangea adds structure.*

PLANT SPECIFICS

In the Home Garden

Wildflower planting becomes more
popular each year, and firms
offer bulk seeds for such uses as
scattering in meadows, highway
beautification, and conservation.
Flowers that spread and naturalize,
whether native or imported,
are obviously plants that do
not require much care. If you have
suitable sites, even those you
consider problem areas, you might
try some of the naturalized plants
that have prospered at Winterthur,
such as cup plant or swamp
aster. For cultivated beds, hibiscus
moscheutos, white eupatorium, or
wreath goldenrod make fine additions
and offer flower-arranging
material as well.

Aster divaricatus

ASTER
Aster
Asteraceae
The two asters described here are native
to eastern North America. Both herbaceous
perennials. Zones 3–8.

    A. divaricatus (white wood aster),
white daisy-type flowers in late summer, fall.
Propagation: self-sows. Size 1'–2' tall, equal
spread. Soil: moist to dry. Sun to shade.
A. puneceus (swamp aster, or purple-stemmed
aster), lavender daisy-type flowers in midfall.
Useful for damp areas. Self-sows.
Propagation: division, seeds. Size: 3'–6' tall,
equal spread. Soil: consistently moist. Sun.

Daucus carota

DAUCUS CAROTA
Queen Anne's Lace
Umbelliferae
Europe
Herbaceous biennial. Flat, lacy clusters of
white flowers in midsummer; lovely dried
or in flower arrangements. Self-sows;
good for meadows, fields. Size: 2'–3' tall,
equal spread. Soil: dry. Sun. Zones 3–8.

Eupatorium rugosum

EUPATORIUM RUGOSUM
White Snakeroot
Asteraceae
Eastern N. America
Herbaceous perennial. Clusters of fuzzy,
white flowers in fall. Spreads by rhizomes and
self-seeding; may become invasive. Cut back
after flowering to prevent seed drop. Size:
3'–5' tall, 4' spread. Soil: moist, well drained,
fertile. Sun to light shade. Zones 3–7.

HIBISCUS MOSCHEUTOS
Swamp Rose Mallow
Malvaceae
Eastern U.S.
Tall, herbaceous perennial. Large red, pink,
or white flowers in late summer. Native to

Hibiscus moscheutos

marshes and streamsides; will grow in good garden soil with consistent moisture. Propagation: seed or cuttings. Cultivars, some with ruffled petals. Size: 3'–7' tall, 3'–4' spread. Soil: moist to wet. Sun. Zones 5–9.

MYOSOTIS SCORPIOIDES
Forget-Me-Not
Boraginaceae
Europe, Asia
Herbaceous perennial. Soft, sky blue flowers in early summer. Grows naturally in water. Cultivars available. Propagation: division or seeds. Size: 6"–8" tall, 8" spread. Soil: constant moisture. Sun or partial shade. Zones 3–8.

Myosotis scorpioides

SILPHIUM PERFOLIATUM
Cup Plant
Asteraceae
Midwestern U.S.
Herbaceous perennial; tall, robust. Yellow daisylike blossoms in midsummer. Leaves hold water. Easy. Self-seeds. Size: 3'–6' tall, 4'–5' spread. Soil: moist to dry. Sun to partial shade. Zones 3–8 (9).

Silphium perfoliatum

SOLIDAGO CAESIA
Wreath Goldenrod
Asteraceae
Eastern N. America

Solidago caesia

Herbaceous perennial. Golden yellow flowers along arching stems in fall. Easy. Propagation: seeds or division of rhizomes in spring. European hybridizers have developed excellent garden goldenrods based on our native plants. Size: 1'–3' tall, 1'–2' spread. Soil: moist to dry. Sun to partial shade. Zones 3–8 (9).

BERRIES AND FALL-BLOOMING BULBS
July–November

BERRIES

By mid August, berries are noticeable everywhere. Part of nature's bounty, they add another dimension to gardens in early fall. Most berries attract birds; in fact, some are so appealing that they are rarely seen in their ripened state. Others last much of the winter.

One of the most outstanding berry displays is that of the kousa dogwood *(Cornus kousa)*, the same tree that in June featured great "frosted" branches of blossoms. In late August and early September, these trees are laden with pendulous, rosy red fruits that resemble raspberries and are edible, although not very tasty. Birds like them, however, and the fruits gradually

Near an entrance to Winterthur's Enchanted Woods™, purple berries of Callicarpa japonica *and yellow berries of* Viburnum *'Michael Dodge' harmonize with golden fall foliage.*

disappear. Our native dogwood (*C. florida*) is no slouch either, producing shiny red berries in clusters of three or four during August and September.

Other champion berry producers include the vast genus of viburnums. Among the most beautiful are the orange-cast berries of the siebold viburnum (*V. sieboldii*) that appear in late July, just in time to combine with franklinia or other July-blooming plants. Also outstanding is *V. nudum* 'Winterthur,' with berries that turn from green to white, then pink, and finally blue. Sometimes all colors appear at the same time in one bunch. This viburnum has glossy green leaves that become rich burgundy later in the fall.

Yellow berries are rarer, but *V. dilatatum* 'Michael Dodge' has them in abundance. Linden viburnum, the

Pairing Viburnum nudum *'Winterthur' and* V. nudum *will ensure a good berry set.*

species of which 'Michael Dodge' is a cultivar, has shiny red berries that last until late winter. Tea viburnum (*V. setigerum*) bears showy clusters of hanging, oval fruits that turn orange-red in September and last into late fall.

Sapphireberry (*Symplocos paniculata*) is well named, featuring stunning blue berries that disappear about as fast as real sapphires would. Stewartias produce interesting fruits, many with "beaks," such as the *S. rostrata* capsules that turn rosy red in July. That same month, fragrant snowbell (*Styrax obassia*) produces pale green berries that look like bunches of grapes. Hardy orange (*Poncirus trifoliata*) develops golden fruits of golfball size. This thorny shrub is sometimes used as barrier hedging.

Jewel-like violet berries that last from September through November are the most striking feature of beauty-berries (*Callicarpa*) and are worth the wait. *Callicarpa dichotoma* is low and spreading and makes a good "facing-down" plant when grown in front of others. The berries are displayed along arching branches, their color emphasizing the plant's gracefulness. *C. japonica* is more vase shaped and has clusters of berries in the same deep, royal violet tone. The name *callicarpa* comes from two Greek words that mean, as you may guess, "beautiful fruit."

FALL-BLOOMING BULBS

Three fall-blooming bulbous plants are noteworthy, all featuring chalicelike blossoms. First is showy colchicum (*Colchicum speciosum*), sometimes called autumn crocus, although it is not a true crocus. On Oak Hill, colchicum

A mass planting of Colchicum speciosum, *here growing on Winterthur's Oak Hill, will brighten September gardens.*

is planted in grass, which is important for its effectiveness since the foliage comes in spring and dies down by midsummer. When cut, colchicum will last in water for several days.

Another plant with a misleading common name is *Sternbergia lutea*. Known as fall daffodil, its rich yellow blossoms look more like crocuses than daffodils, yet it is neither. Perhaps it is best to use the Latin *sternbergia* and honor the Austrian botanist for whom the plant is named. It features strap-shape foliage that accompa-

nies the blossoms, which are attractive with the colors of autumn leaves. Sternbergia is also excellent with the berries of callicarpas, hardy orange, and tea viburnum, with which it is grouped on Oak Hill.

Showy crocus *(Crocus speciosus)*, a third fall-blooming plant, really is what its common name implies: a crocus. Easy to grow, it has bluish lavender petals and bright orange stigmas that are much divided. It blooms when the foliage is very short; after blooming, the foliage continues to elongate.

In the Home Garden

It is easy to be carried away by a plant when it is in full bloom. However, to keep a garden interesting all year, two-, three-, or four-season plants are certainly desirable. Dogwoods Cornus kousa and C. florida are wonderful in this regard, with their beautiful blossoms, foliage, fall fruits and color, and great winter architecture. Stewartias are similarly valuable.

Almost any garden can offer a place for the fall-blooming bulbs described here. These plants add ground-hugging color to vistas featuring fall foliage and berries. Or you might plant some by your front door as a welcoming committee.

In this section, I use the term *berry* loosely, since botanists differentiate fruits, naming them *drupes, capsules,* and *pomes* (among other designations), depending on their structure. Similarly, the term *bulb* here includes both bulbs and corms.

Callicarpa japonica

CALLICARPA
Beauty-Berry
Verbenaceae

These two species are deciduous and of easy culture. Showy, violet fruit in fall. Pinkish lavender flowers, not showy. Can be cut back in spring; blooms on new wood. Propagation: softwood cuttings. Soil: well drained.
C. dichotoma (purple beauty-berry), China, Japan. Fruit along arching branches. Size: 3'–4' tall, equal spread. Sun. Zones 5–8.
C. japonica (Japanese beauty-berry), Japan. Vase-shape shrub. Clusters of fruit. Size: 4'–6' tall, equal spread. Sun to light shade. Zones 5–8.

COLCHICUM SPECIOSUM
Showy Colchicum
Liliaceae
Turkey

Colchicum speciosum

Corm. Pinkish lavender, crocuslike flowers in early fall. Flowers need foliage of other plants because spring-blooming straplike foliage dies down in summer. Trouble free. Propagation: seed or offsets. Many other colchicum species and cultivars. Size: 4"–6" tall, equal spread. Soil: rich, well drained. Partial shade to full sun. Zones 5–7.

CORNUS
Dogwood
Cornaceae

Here are two deciduous dogwood trees (one is native). Outstanding multiseason plants. Propagation: softwood cuttings. Soil:

Cornus kousa

acid, moist, well drained, organically rich. Sun to partial shade. *C. florida* (flowering dogwood), eastern U.S. and Mexico. In early spring, showy white bracts surround the true flowers, making this native tree an all-time favorite. Beautiful horizontal branching. Clusters of shiny red berries in early fall; excellent fall foliage. Innumerable cultivars. Size: 20'–40' tall, equal spread. Zones (5) 6–9. *C. kousa* (kousa dogwood), Japan, Korea, China. Outstanding in late-spring bloom, when white flower bracts cover spreading branches. Raspberry-like fruit in early fall. Trouble free. Many cultivars. Size: 20'–30' tall, equal spread. Zones 5–8.

Crocus speciosus

CROCUS SPECIOSUS
Showy Crocus
Iridaceae
Russia, Turkey
Corm. Lavender chalicelike flowers with conspicuous orange stigmas in midautumn. Bladelike leaves. Can be grown in grass. Propagation: produces offsets; self-seeds. Cultivars available. Size: 4"–6" tall, 6" spread. Soil: adaptable. Sun. Zones (4) 5–7 (8).

Poncirus trifoliata

PONCIRUS TRIFOLIATA
Hardy Orange
Rutaceae
China, Korea
Deciduous shrub. White, single flowers in midspring. Showy, golden yellow fruit ripens during fall. Sharp thorns. Trouble free. Propagation: seeds, cuttings. Size: 8'–20' tall, 5'–15' spread. Soil: acid (though adaptable), well drained. Sun. Zones (5) 6–9.

STERNBERGIA LUTEA
Fall Daffodil
Amaryllidaceae
Mediterranean region

Sternbergia lutea

Bulb. Rich yellow, crocuslike flowers and straplike foliage in fall. Needs hot, baking sun in summer. Trouble free. Size: 6"–10" tall, equal spread. Soil: adaptable. Sun. Zones 6–9.

Stewartia rostrata

STEWARTIA ROSTRATA
Stewartia Rostrata
Theaceae
China
Deciduous tree. White, cupped flowers and lustrous green foliage in midspring. Beaked, rosy red fruit by midsummer. Trouble free. Little pruning required. Size: 15' tall, equal spread. Soil: acid, moist, well drained, high organic. Partial shade. Zones 6–7.

STYRAX OBASSIA
Fragrant Snowbell
Styracaceae
Japan, Korea
Deciduous tree. Flowers in graceful, white, hanging racemes in late spring. Pale green fruit by midsummer. Propagation: softwood

Styrax obassia

cuttings in July. Size: 20'–30' tall, 15'–25'
spread. Soil: acid, moist, well drained,
high organic. Sun to partial shade. Zones 5–8.

SYMPLOCOS PANICULATA
Sapphireberry
Symplocaceae
Himalayas, China, Japan
Small, deciduous tree. Fuzzy, creamy white,
fragrant flowers in late spring. Brilliant blue
fruit in early fall. Needs mate to assure fruit
set. Trouble free. Prune in winter if needed.
Propagation: softwood cuttings. Size: 10'–20'
tall, equal spread. Soil: acid, well drained.
Sun to light shade. Zones 4–8.

Symplocos paniculata

Viburnum dilatatum 'Michael Dodge'

VIBURNUM
Viburnum
Caprifoliaceae
Here are five viburnums; all excellent berry
producers. Upright, deciduous shrubs.
Flowers bloom as creamy, flat clusters in late
spring/early summer. Dependable, easy
to grow. Cultivars available. Sun to partial
shade. Propagation: softwood cuttings.
Prune in late fall.

    V. dilatatum (linden viburnum), Asia.
Shiny red fruit lasts through most of winter.
More than one plant needed for good fruit
set. Size: 8'–10' tall, 5'–7' spread. Soil: moist,
well drained, slightly acid. Zones (4) 5–7.
V. dilatatum **'Michael Dodge'** (Michael
Dodge viburnum), yellow fruit. *V. nudum*
'Winterthur' (Winterthur viburnum),
species: eastern U.S. Lustrous green foliage
turns rich burgundy in fall. Fruit changes
from green to white, then pink, finally blue.
Needs a species *V. nudum* for good berry
set. Size: 6' tall, 5' spread. Soil: acid, tolerates
damp. Zones 5–9. *V. setigerum* (tea viburnum),
China. Orange-red fruit in clusters; decorative.
Size: 8'–12' tall, 5'–8' spread. Soil: moist,
well drained, slightly acid. Zones 5–7 (8).

Viburnum nudum 'Winterthur'

V. sieboldii (siebold viburnum), Japan. Large
shrub or tree. Handsome, textured leaves.
Showy orange fruit turns black. Size: 15'–20'
tall, 10'–15' spread. Soil: moist, well drained,
pH adaptable. Zones 4–7 (8).

Viburnum setigerum

Photinia villosa *on Winterthur's Oak Hill adds soft apricot to the colors of the woodlands.*

FALL FOLIAGE
August–November

In autumn nature puts on her party clothes for one last fling. With seeming abandon, she combines all kinds of hues—bright and striking, soft and muted—for a many-splendored effect. Whole trees become tinted; big shrubs are saturated so that our surroundings are perhaps more colorful than at any other time of year. Although this panorama proceeds apace with no help from us, when planning our properties we can certainly give thought to including trees and shrubs with enjoyable fall color. Many are of simple culture.

One of the earliest signs of fall is the appearance in late August of the soft, rosy red tips on the branches of burning bush *(Euonymus alatus)*. The color gradually permeates the whole shrub, which becomes a spectacular autumn display. Since burning bush holds its leaves for a long time, the color lasts through much of the season. Deservedly popular, it is easy to grow, makes a good screen, and its corky branches offer winter interest. We may choose either the large size of the species or the somewhat smaller cultivars.

Also coloring early is our native dogwood (*Cornus florida*), which takes on russet tones in September. Mixtures of red, green, yellow, and purple in the leaves, combined with red berries, give this handsome tree various effects depending on the sunlight. Meanwhile, Korean stewartia (*Stewartia koreana*), a rich red tree of splendid stature, stands like a sentinel at the entrance to Winterthur's Visitor Parking Area. Its glorious color lasts about six weeks. By mid October, the woods are alive with the clear bright yellow of our native spice-

In autumn, Enkianthus perulatus *becomes a rich red accent at Magnolia Bend.*

bush (*Lindera benzoin*), a smallish shrub that makes up in brilliance what it lacks in size. Another shrub found throughout the woodlands is oriental photinia (*Photinia villosa*), which grows in a graceful vase shape and bears delicate apricot leaves.

Some shrubs have their best season in autumn. Fothergilla, for example, really outdoes itself with vibrant shades of yellow, orange, and scarlet—often on the same plant, even on the same leaf. It colors fairly late in the season, in late October and early November, in the Sundial Garden at Winterthur. Two species, *F. major* and *F. gardenii*, offer a choice of sizes. A more unusual shrub, but equally outstanding for fall coloration, is white enkianthus (*Enkianthus perulatus*). Handsome year-round, with good habit and white, bell-like blossoms in spring, it is truly striking in autumn, when leaves turn a brilliant red. It is not common in the trade but worth searching for. Bridalwreath spirea (*Spiraea prunifolia*), another inhabitant of the Sundial Garden, has two special seasons. Spring brings sprays of white, buttonlike flowers, whereas fairly late in autumn, the leaves turn a lovely apricot color.

Several large native trees are exciting at this time of year as well. Red maple (*Acer rubrum*) and sugar maple (*A. saccharum*) are well known for their last hurrah of brilliant yellow, orange, and red. Our native sour gum (*Nyssa sylvatica*) offers red, orange, yellow, and purple tints early in the season. Also native and outstanding in the fall are the yellow papaw tree (*Asimina triloba*) and brilliant yellow witch hazel (*Hamamelis virginiana*), which grow together at the entrance to Enchanted Woods™.

Careful planning in the placement of the papaw tree (Asimina triloba) *and witch hazel* (Hamamelis virginiana) *is evident in the fall.*

For late fall color, Sargent cherries *(Prunus sargentii)* present shades and tints of soft red and apricot after many plants have dropped their leaves. The Winterhazel Walk becomes a focal point at Winterthur, as the Korean rhododendron *(R. mucronulatum)* produces colors ranging from plum and apricot to burnt orange. Accompanying this display are the golden tints of corylopsis (*Corylopsis* species and cultivars), making the scene a rich tapestry. Nearby a cut-leaf Japanese maple (*Acer palmatum* var. *dissectum)* is stunning in burnt orange. Meanwhile, giant tulip-poplars, beeches, hickories, and ashes have turned yellow, bronze, and golden tones, brightening our garden walks and inviting us into the woods, which have become a wonderland of color.

In the Home Garden

A wealth of plants offer brilliant fall color for our own domains. Perhaps some of the best shrubs for the home property are the two species of fothergilla. Easy to grow and commendable at all seasons, these shrubs are superb in the fall. Also consider the burning bush, which is well known to most gardeners as a practical, beautiful, and easy-to-grow shrub. The oriental photinia seems to be trouble free in the woods of the estate, and its color is most appealing.

The native spice-bush brightens the woodlands with its high-spirited yellow.

As for trees, Nyssa sylvatica, another native, is as beautiful as its name. It colors early and is exceptional at this season. Probably needing no advertising is the native Cornus florida. All of these plants have stood the test of time at Winterthur, and any would be a fine addition to your fall landscape.

Acer rubrum

ACER
Maple
Aceraceae

These three deciduous trees, one exotic specimen tree and two native shade trees, all have brilliant fall foliage.

A. palmatum **var.** *dissectum* (cut-leaf Japanese maple), Japan, China, Korea. Small tree or shrub. Reddish foliage of finely cut leaves turns burnt orange in late fall. Slow growing. Many cultivars. Propagation difficult. Size: 6'–12' tall, equal spread (cultivars may vary). Soil: moist, well drained, acidic. Sun to dappled shade. Zones (5) 6–8. *A. rubrum* (red maple, swamp maple), eastern U.S. Deciduous tree. Reddish flowers in earliest spring. Excellent fall coloration in yellow, orange, red. Tolerates moist soil. Propagation: softwood cuttings, seeds. Many cultivars. Size: 40'–60' tall, equal spread. Soil: moist, slightly acid, tolerant. Sun. Zones 3–9. *A. saccharum* (sugar maple), eastern Canada and U.S. Majestic deciduous tree. Greenish yellow flowers in spring, before leaves.

Acer saccharum

Glorious fall coloration, yellow to orange to red. Propagation: softwood cuttings. Many cultivars. Size: 60'–75' tall, 40'–60' spread. Soil: moist, well drained, fertile, pH adaptable. Sun to partial shade. Zones 4–8.

ASIMINA TRILOBA
Papaw
Annonaceae
Eastern and Midwestern U.S.

Deciduous tree. Inconspicuous purple flowers in midspring. Brilliant yellow foliage in fall. Fruits, foliage colors vary. Pest free. Transplanting difficult. Propagation: difficult. Size: 15'–30' tall, equal spread. Soil: moist, well drained, fertile, slightly acid. Sun to partial shade. Zones 5–8.

CORNUS FLORIDA
Flowering Dogwood
For detailed information, see "Azalea Woods" (page 72).

CORYLOPSIS
SPECIES AND CULTIVARS
For detailed information, see "Winterhazel Walk" (page 27).

ENKIANTHUS PERULATUS
White Enkianthus
Ericaceae
Japan
Deciduous, rounded shrub. White, urn-shape flowers. Outstanding red color in fall. Size:

Enkianthus perulatus

4'–6' tall, equal spread. Soil: acid, moist, well drained. Sun to partial shade. Zones 5–7.

Euonymus alatus

EUONYMUS ALATUS
Burning Bush
Celastraceae
Asia
Deciduous shrub. Yellow-green inconspicuous flowers in late spring; red-colored foliage in early autumn, lasts well. Trouble free. Cultivars of somewhat smaller size available. Propagation: softwood cuttings. Soil: well drained, adaptable. Size: 15'–20' tall, 18'–25' spread. Sun or shade. Zones 4–8 (9).

FOTHERGILLA
Fothergilla
Hamamelidaceae
For detailed information, see "Sundial Garden" (page 64).

HAMAMELIS VIRGINIANA
Common Witch Hazel
Hamamelidaceae
Eastern N. America
Deciduous shrub. Fragrant, yellow, fringelike blossoms appear with yellow fall foliage. Problem free, dependable. Prune after flowering. Propagation: softwood cuttings. Size: 15'–20' tall, 10'–15' spread. Soil: moist. Sun or shade. Zones 3–8 (9).

Lindera benzoin

LINDERA BENZOIN
Spice-bush
Lauraceae
Eastern U.S.
Deciduous shrub; problem free. Graceful

habit. Modest yellow flowers appear before leaves. Yellow fall color. Prune after flowering. Propagation: seed. Size: 6'–12' tall, equal spread. Soil: moist, well drained, acid but adaptable. Sun to shade. Zones 4–9.

Nyssa sylvatica

NYSSA SYLVATICA
Sour Gum, Black Gum
Nyssaceae
Eastern U.S.

Deciduous tree. Greenish yellow flowers bloom with leaves in spring. Lustrous foliage turns red, yellow, orange, purple, in early fall.

Propagation: difficult. Some cultivars. Size: 30'–50' tall, 20'–30' spread. Soil: acid, moist, well drained. Sun to partial shade. Zones 4–9.

PHOTINIA VILLOSA
Oriental Photinia
Rosaceae
Japan, Korea, China

Deciduous, vase-shape shrub. White flowers in late spring. Apricot fall coloration. Little pruning required. Propagation: softwood and hardwood cuttings. Size: 10'–15' tall, 8'–10' spread. Soil: acid, moist, well drained. Sun to partial shade. Zones 4–7.

Prunus sargentii

PRUNUS SARGENTII
Sargent Cherry
Rosaceae
Japan

Handsome, huge deciduous tree. Single, white flowers turn pink, appear before leaves. Apricot fall color. Propagation: softwood cuttings. Size: 20'–50' tall, equal spread. Soil: adaptable. Sun. Zones 4–7.

Rhododendron mucronulatum

RHODODENDRON MUCRONULATUM
Korean Rhododendron
Ericaceae
China, Korea, Japan

Deciduous shrub. Fall foliage ranges from plum to apricot to burnt orange. Rosy lavender flowers appear before leaves. Trouble free. Prune after flowering. Propagation: seed, softwood cuttings. Several cultivars, including 'Cornell Pink.' Size: 4'–8' tall, equal spread. Soil: acid, moist, well drained, organically rich. Partial shade. Zones 4–7.

Spiraea prunifolia

SPIRAEA PRUNIFOLIA
Bridalwreath Spirea
Rosaceae
Asia
Deciduous shrub. Adaptable, trouble free.
Double, white, buttonlike flowers in early
spring. Apricot fall foliage. Prune after
flowering. Propagation: softwood or hard-
wood cuttings. Size: 4'–9' tall, 6'–8' spread.
Soil: any good garden. Sun. Zones 4–8.

Stewartia koreana

STEWARTIA KOREANA
Korean Stewartia
Theaceae
Korea
Deciduous tree. Nice habit, excellent fall
color. White, cup-shape flowers in early
summer; round buds. Trouble free. Little
pruning required. Propagation: June
cuttings. Cultivars available. Size: 20'–30' tall,
equal spread. Soil: acid, moist, well drained,
organically rich. Sun to partial shade.
Zones 5–7.

ASIAN PLANTS

Spiraea prunifolium and *Stewartia koreana* are but two of the myriad
plants in this book that are native to Asia. Asian countries benefited
from more favorable conditions during the Ice Ages and thus offer
a tantalizing wealth of plants, whereas many species on other conti-
nents perished. Intrepid explorers endured hardships and even risked
their lives to bring to Europe and North America specimens of these
Asian treasures that we now enjoy in our gardens. Plant exploration
worldwide forms a fascinating chapter in horticultural history.

⁓⁓⊰⊱⁓⁓

"I was born here and get more
enthusiastic each year about
every portion of the grounds and
house. . . . Living here all year
round I always try to have flowers
that bloom the very earliest and
the very latest. In fact, on the
terrace near my house there
is always a flower blooming
each month of the year."

—*H. F. du Pont, 1937*

⁓⁓⊰⊱⁓⁓

Winter

*"Heavy snow so as to make
old trees beautiful."*

—*H. F. du Pont, Garden Diary, 1911*

Few things are more beautiful than the countryside after a snowfall.
We enjoy the exquisite branching of deciduous trees, the graceful
proportions of evergreens, the quiet serenity. But without new snow
to create a winter wonderland, we may wish for enlivening details
to counteract a more somber landscape. Adding color to the winter
garden takes only a little ingenuity, and these pages provide a variety
of effective ways to meet the challenge. Hollies, uncommon conifers,
and winter-blooming plants are described. You will also find suggestions
for enjoying color inside.

*Opener: Henry Algernon du Pont, Henry Francis's father, began Winterthur's
Pinetum, an extensive collection of conifers, in 1918. Today these stately
evergreens serve as a year-round backdrop for the changing garden scenes.*

Left: Ilex opaca

HOLIDAY CHEER
December

Winter is a time of celebration. Hollies and conifers, invaluable for providing color in the winter landscape, also furnish choice material for decorating our homes as winter festivities begin.

HOLLIES

Hollies are wonderful plants for landscaping—they offer many sizes, shapes, and textures and maintain their good looks year-round. Yet in December these plants really come into their own. They seem to enjoy winter weather, bringing life and color to gardens when many plants have lost their leaves or are curled up against the cold.

Various hollies provide lustrous green leaves and red berries for decorations inside and out. Many types have leaves of great substance that last well when cut, and branches may be cut anytime without ill effect. Unlike most broad-leaved evergreens, hollies thrive in sunny as well as shady spots. Hundreds of cultivars are available, and there is one suitable for nearly every purpose in a wide range of climates. With few exceptions, hollies

are dioecious, meaning that both male and female plants are needed for berry production, which occurs on female plants.

Winterthur, an American country estate, appropriately features American holly *(Ilex opaca)*, with its pyramidal shape, characteristic pointed leaves, and red berries. Since the berries form on the current year's

Stately American hollies grow near the musuem and throughout the estate.

Paperbark maple (Acer griseum) *is a standout in the snow.*

growth (that is, near the ends of the branches), the branches are valuable for decorative purposes. American hollies appear throughout the estate. The cultivar of a deciduous species, Winter Red winterberry holly (*Ilex verticillata* 'Winter Red'), grows near the museum and produces sprays of red berries on silvery branches.

In the Sundial Garden, other hollies delineate sections and provide green in every season.

CONIFERS

Needled evergreens, or conifers, also bring life to December gardens and, like hollies, provide excellent

In Winterthur's Sundial Garden, hollies such as Ilex glabra *'Compacta' delineate sections and provide green in every season.*

decorating material. The Pinetum offers a range of beautiful specimens. Among them, the Japanese umbrella pine *(Sciadopitys verticillata)* is noteworthy for a small property. This slow grower features long, glossy needles that maintain their dark green color all winter. The tree is pest free and adds an interesting texture to the landscape. Cut branches last well in water.

Another conifer to consider for the home garden is the Japanese cryptomeria *(Cryptomeria japonica)*, a graceful, pyramidal tree with soft, feathery texture. Several grow at Winterthur between the Reflecting Pool and the Research Building. The beautiful, reddish brown bark can sometimes be seen through the branches. Needles are brighter green in summer than in winter, when they occasionally take on a bronzy hue, especially if affected by wind.

The blue atlas cedar *(Cedrus atlantica* 'Glauca') is a striking conifer that in time becomes much larger than the two trees just mentioned. Although rather open and rangy and tending to be pyramidal in adolescence, it matures into a full, rounded tree with silvery blue needles and distinctive texture. Always eye catching, this tree is exceptionally attractive against stone or other gray-tone materials that complement its natural hue.

DECIDUOUS TREES

The bark and branching patterns of deciduous trees can also be assets in the winter scene. Paperbark maple *(Acer griseum)* is arresting at this season, with cinnamon-colored exfoliating bark and fine architecture. This handsome tree offers good fall foliage color and makes an excellent specimen plant.

PLANT SPECIFICS

In the Home Garden

Any of these plants would bring welcome color to your landscape or home during the winter season. Some are common, others less so, but all are relatively easy to grow. Plants that tolerate damp soil are fairly rare and nice to know about. Two of the hollies discussed above, Ilex glabra *and* I. verticillata, *qualify.*

Acer griseum

ACER GRISEUM
Paperbark Maple
Aceraceae
China
Vase-shape deciduous tree. Cinnamon-colored exfoliating bark; excellent fall foliage. Propagation: difficult. Size: 20'–30' tall, 15'–20' spread. Soil: moist, well drained, pH adaptable. Sun to partial shade. Zones 5–7 (8).

CEDRUS ATLANTICA 'GLAUCA'
Blue Atlas Cedar
Pinaceae
Algeria, Morocco (Atlas Mountains)
Majestic evergreen tree; outstanding in the landscape. Silvery blue needles. Propagation: cuttings of firm tip shoots, late fall. Size: 40'–60' tall, 30'–40' spread. Soil: moist, well drained, acid, though pH adaptable. Sun to partial shade. Zones 6–8 (9).

Cedrus atlantica 'Glauca'

CRYPTOMERIA JAPONICA
Japanese Cryptomeria
Taxodiaceae
China, Japan
Pyramidal evergreen. Graceful sprays of green needles in summer; may bronze in winter in windy sites. Easy. Propagation:

Cryptomeria japonica

cuttings in November. Many cultivars. Size: 50'–60' tall, 20'–30' spread. Soil: acid, moist, well drained, light. Sun to partial shade. Zones (5) 6–8.

ILEX
Holly
Aquifoliaceae
Three evergreen and one deciduous holly are grouped here. Prune at any time of year. Propagation: softwood cuttings.

    I. crenata **'Microphylla'** (Microphylla Japanese holly), species from Asia. Shrub. Small, pointed, evergreen leaves, glossy and leathery. Grown for foliage. Many other cultivars. Size: 8'–12' tall, equal spread. Soil: moist, well drained, slightly acid. Sun or shade. Zones (5) 6–7 (8). *I. glabra* **'Compacta'** (dwarf inkberry holly), species from eastern N. America. Shrub; rather upright. Small, glossy evergreen leaves. Grown for foliage. Problem free. Many other cultivars. Size: 4'–6' tall, equal spread. Soil: acid, can be damp; adaptable. Sun or shade. Zones 4–9. *I. opaca* (American holly), eastern U.S. Large shrub or tree. Evergreen foliage; red berries (female plants) in early winter. Slow growing. Many excellent cultivars. Size: 15'–30' tall, 10'–20' spread. Soil: moist, well drained, acid. Sun to partial shade. Zones 5–9. *I. verticillata* **'Winter Red'**

Ilex opaca

(Winter Red winterberry), species from eastern U.S. and Canada. Deciduous shrub. Profuse red berries (female plant) in fall, winter. Problem free. Many other excellent cultivars. Size: 6'–10' tall, equal spread. Soil: moist (will tolerate wet), acid. Sun to partial shade. Zones 3–9.

Sciadopitys verticillata

SCIADOPITYS VERTICILLATA
Japanese Umbrella Pine
Pinaceae
Japan
Slow-growing evergreen. Long, glossy, dark green needles retain color throughout winter. Unusual texture. Pest free. Propagation: winter or summer cuttings. Size: 20'–30' tall, 15'–20' spread. Sun. Soil: acid, moist, well drained, organically rich. Zones 5–7.

A WINTER GARDEN
January–April

If you have a bit of masonry that catches the winter sun and thus warms the ground nearby, you may want to plan a winter garden similar to that on Winterthur's East Terrace. There, plants with early and overlapping bloom times offer combinations of white, yellow, lavender, and blue flowers from January to April. Rarely the same from year to year because of the vagaries of winter weather, this variability lends interest and is part of the garden's charm.

Blooming on the terrace are three tiny plants that will fit almost anywhere: white snowdrops (*Galanthus* species), yellow adonis (*Adonis amurensis*), and lavender Tommies (*Crocus tommasinianus*). Among the earliest winter-into-spring flowers, they grow together in a little bed, sheltered by masonry and under shrubs that bloom companionably. One such shrub is Chinese witch hazel (*Hamamelis mollis*), which every February produces yellow flowers with straplike petals that look like bits of fringe. Prized for its unusual bloom time, it is also valued for its handsome habit and brilliant yellow fall foliage. The cultivar growing on the terrace is Princeton Gold.

The winter garden on Winterthur's East Terrace groups adonis, snowdrops, and Tommies with Princeton Gold witch hazel.

Chionodoxa and Pieris japonica (background) *bloom together in earliest spring.*

Also blooming here in winter is fragrant honey-suckle *(Lonicera fragrantissima)*, a shrub with creamy blossoms that flower over a long period. Both witch hazel and honeysuckle offer fragrance: the witch hazel is subtle and pleasant; the honeysuckle, living up to the promise of *fragrantissima*, is mesmerizing. Trailing branches of winter jasmine *(Jasminum nudiflorum)* hang from a nearby balustrade, where it produces yellow, open-face, tubular blossoms on warm days and continues to bloom into spring. In the home garden, you might allow winter jasmine to ramble over a retaining wall or let it grow into the branches of a dark evergreen (since the flowers appear before the foliage). Reinforcing the yellow theme, a cornelian cherry dogwood tree (*Cornus mas*) sends out airy blossoms over all. Later a large corylopsis shrub (*Corylopsis pauciflora*) blooms with paler yellow, bell-like blossoms.

Two bulbous plants grow in the lawn on the terrace. Very early to appear are Tommies, which have formed a flourishing colony. Lavender and silvery petals and orange stigmas blend to produce drifts of a most beautiful hue. Later, glory-of-the-snow (*Chionodoxa forbesii*) forms sheets of bright lavender blue flowers that make a striking display when combined with the yellows, creams, and spring greens nearby.

Broadleaved evergreens also play a role here, adding solidity and year-round green. Two with timely bloom are Japanese pieris (*Pieris japonica*) and sweet-box (*Sarcococca hookeriana* var. *humilis*). Japanese pieris is a sizable shrub with glossy foliage and hanging clusters of white flowers that open in early spring. Sweet-box, a much smaller plant, also has lustrous green leaves and tiny, sweet-smelling, creamy blossoms. Southern magnolia (*Magnolia grandiflora*) and American holly (*Ilex opaca*) grow on the terrace as well.

WITCH HAZEL

Witch hazels (*Hamamelis* species and hybrids) deserve special mention as candidates for a winter garden. They are so reliable as February-blooming plants that many are used in Winterthur's public reception areas to supply color and encouragement during the final stretch of winter.

Several Pallida Chinese witch hazels (*H. mollis* 'Pallida') are prominent at the Visitor Center and near the Galleries. The bloom—soft sulfur yellow and profuse—lasts for several weeks. As its name suggests, Pallida is a lighter yellow than the species, which also grows at the Visitor Center. Other February bloomers include hybrid witch hazels (*H.* x *intermedia*), whose blossoms range from yellow to copper and red tones, depending on the cultivar. They offer orange to red fall coloration, and all display hybrid vigor. In the Quarry Garden, Jelena and Diane cultivars bloom in soft

Diane witch hazel (Hamamelis *x* intermedia *'Diane') growing below Winterthur's Quarry Garden, unfurls coppery red flowers in February.*

coppery and red tones. These are lovely, too, but are not as showy as the yellow types.

You might find appealing two native witch hazels that have fragrant blossoms and are a little hardier than those described above. Common witch hazel *(H. virginiana)* produces yellow flowers in November, when its foliage is also turning yellow (see "Fall Foliage," page 139). This handsome shrub reaches a height of 15'–20' or more. Vernal witch hazel *(H. vernalis)* grows 6'–10' tall and starts to bloom here in December, following its autumn coloring. The flowers range from yellow to red and mixtures thereof and persist three to four weeks. These two native witch hazels will tolerate damp situations.

Magnolia grandiflora *prospers in a sheltered spot on the East Terrace.*

PLANT SPECIFICS

In the Home Garden

Winter gardens can be small and intimate, offering glimpses of color to be enjoyed "up close and personal" during spells when the weather eases.

A south-facing retaining wall or a stone outcropping can provide an ideal place to plant a few of the hardy souls mentioned here. For a larger, more eye-catching winter display, consider adding a few shrubs or trees, such as witch hazel, fragrant honeysuckle, or Cornus mas. *The south side of your house or a walled-in terrace could be a suitable site. Other plants that H. F. du Pont used from time to time on the terrace were Christmas rose* (Helleborus niger), *crocus species* C. chrysanthus *and* C. imperati, *white periwinkle* (Vinca minor *'Alba'*), *and sweet violets* (Viola odorata).

ADONIS AMURENSIS
Amur Adonis
For detailed information, see "March Bank" (page 20).

CHIONODOXA FORBESII
(FORMERLY C. LUCILIAE)
Glory-of-the-Snow
For detailed information, see "March Bank" (page 20).

Cornus mas

CORNUS MAS
Cornelian Cherry Dogwood
Cornaceae
Europe, Western Asia
Deciduous tree. Ethereal flowers in yellow clusters on bare branches in early spring. Pest free. Propagation: softwood cuttings. Cultivars available. Size: 20'–25' tall, 20' spread. Soil: neutral, well drained. Sun to partial shade. Zones 4–7 (8).

CORYLOPSIS PAUCIFLORA
Buttercup Winterhazel
For detailed information, see "Winterhazel Walk" (page 27).

CROCUS TOMMASINIANUS
Tommies
Iridaceae
Yugoslavia
Lavender and silver chalice-shape blossoms in earliest spring. Orange stigmas. If grown in a lawn, delay mowing or raise mower to 3" until foliage ripens. Propagation: separation of offsets, seed. Size: 4"–6" tall, 6" spread. Soil: well drained, humus rich. Sun to partial shade. Zones (3) 4–8 (9).

Crocus tommasinianus

GALANTHUS
Snowdrop
Amaryllidaceae
For detailed information, see "March Bank" (page 20). *G. cilicicus* (Cilician snowdrop), from Turkey, is an early-blooming species that du Pont used on the terrace.

HAMAMELIS
Witch Hazel
Hamamelidaceae
Deciduous shrubs; vigorous, dependable. Fringelike blossoms in late fall, winter. Excellent fall foliage. Prune after flowering. Propagation: softwood cuttings. These three

species and a hybrid offer a choice of color, bloom time, size, and hardiness.

H. x _intermedia_ (hybrid witch hazel; _H. japonica_ x _H. mollis_), parents from Asia. Innumerable cultivars, yellow to copper to red flowers in February, before leaves. Fall foliage

Hamamelis x *intermedia* 'Jelena'

in similar hues. Size: 15'–20' tall, equal spread. Soil: moist, well drained, acid. Sun to partial shade. Zones 5–8. **H. mollis** (Chinese witch hazel), China. Yellow flowers in February last for several weeks. Cultivars include _H. mollis_ 'Pallida.' Size: 10'–15' tall, equal spread. Soil: moist, well drained, acid. Sun to partial shade. Zones 5–8. **H. vernalis** (vernal witch hazel), central N. America. Flowers variable (yellow to red) and appear in December. Cultivars available. Size: 6'–10' tall, 8'–12' spread. Soil: moist, pH adaptable. Sun to partial shade. Zones 4–8. **H. virginiana** (common witch hazel), eastern N. America. Yellow flowers and foliage in November. Size: 15'–20' tall, 10'–15' spread. Soil: moist. Sun or shade. Zones 3–8 (9).

ILEX OPACA
American Holly
For detailed information, see "Holiday Cheer" (page 150).

JASMINUM NUDIFLORUM
Winter Jasmine
Oleaceae
China

Deciduous shrub; trailing branches. Yellow flowers on warm winter days, before leaves. Prune after flowering. Propagation: cuttings. Size: 3'–4' tall (to 15' tall, with support). Soil: adaptable. Sun or shade. Zones 6–10.

Lonicera fragrantissima

LONICERA FRAGRANTISSIMA
Fragrant Honeysuckle
Caprifoliaceae
China

Deciduous shrub. Creamy white, fragrant flowers and leaves in earliest spring. Prune after flowering. Propagation: cuttings in June. Size: 6' tall, 10' spread. Soil: adaptable, but well drained. Sun to partial shade. Zones 4–8.

MAGNOLIA GRANDIFLORA
Southern Magnolia
For detailed information, see "Magnolia Bend" (page 53).

PIERIS JAPONICA

Japanese Pieris
Ericaceae
Japan, China

Broadleaf evergreen shrub. Hanging clusters of white, urn-shape flowers in early spring. Handsome leathery leaves appear as whorls. Prune after flowering. Propagation: cuttings in fall. Many cultivars. Size: 4'–12' tall, 3'–8' spread. Soil: well drained, acid, high organic. Sun to partial shade. Zones (4) 5–7.

SARCOCOCCA HOOKERIANA VAR. HUMILIS

Sarcococca hookeriana var. *humilis*

Sweet-Box
Buxaceae
China

Small evergreen shrub. Handsome foliage; small, creamy, fragrant flowers in early spring. Problem free. Stoloniferous; can be used as ground cover. Propagation: cuttings in winter. Size: 18"–24" tall, 24" spread. Soil: moist, well drained, acid, high organic. Shade to partial shade. Zones (5) 6–8.

INDOOR BLOOM
February–March

Not one to be caught without an ample supply of flowers for his home, H. F. du Pont used conservatory plants as well as offerings from his twenty-four green-houses to provide winter bloom indoors. He also liked to bring in branches from outdoors that were approaching bloom time and accelerate their flowering with warmth and light (so-called forcing). Here are several suggestions based on these ideas for adding winter color to your home.

TWO CONSERVATORY PLANTS FOR THE HOME

Although greenhouse plants are outside the scope of this book, two outstanding conservatory plants can be recommended for the home gardener. The first is *Clivia miniata* (kaffir lily). An almost indestructible houseplant, it can be neglected for weeks and will not sulk, making it most desirable for busy or forgetful

people. The handsome straplike leaves stay dark green and glossy to their tips; if you cut one, you will find it full of watery fluid, for clivia is one of the camels of the plant world. About once a year, usually in February, the plant produces a glorious, large orange truss (or trusses) or, if you have a rare type, a yellow truss. The incipient bud begins at the plant's neck and slowly rises. After reaching an elegant height, it opens big, lilylike florets, which bloom gradually and last a week or two. Clivias need only moderate light and can last for years, preferring not to be repotted, which is easy.

Camellias *(Camellia japonica)* will also thrive many years in a pot, though they need cool winter conditions (50–60°F), such as in an unheated room, basement, or glassed-in porch. The winter-blooming pink, red, white, or variegated blossoms are among the most exquisite in the plant world and appear during the winter. Deep green leaves—glossy, leathery, and gently curving—are beautiful in their own right. A single blossom floating in a bowl, with accompanying leaves, is a favorite way to enjoy them. During the summer, when the heat and humidity are similar to its natural habitat, the plant can be placed outdoors in the shade. In zones 7 through 9, gardeners can grow these exceptional plants in the ground.

FORCING FLOWERING BRANCHES

In late winter, what could be more enjoyable in your home than an arrangement of spring-flowering branches, whose delicate blossoms and emerging leaves give

Dependable kaffir lily (Clivia miniata) *requires only moderate light and occasional watering.*

Forced branches of quince give evidence that, in Jane Austen's words, "further beauty is known to be at hand."

treatment of shredding the stem ends with pruning shears and placing entire branches in water overnight before standing them in a pail of water for the waiting period. Still others recommend recutting the branches under hot water and adding floral preservative to the pail water. Experimentation is clearly in order, since the process is not exact.

For better texture, a cool place (60–65°F) is recommended. Spraying buds periodically with water is also efficacious. It is necessary to change the pail water weekly until the buds begin to open, at which time the branches should be arranged and brought to their final location. Watching the gradual swelling of the buds is itself great fun.

promise of the season to come? To hasten this pleasurable state, gardeners often cut branches that are nearing their bloom time outdoors and bring them inside, where the branches are "encouraged" (forced) with warmth, water, and light. There, they flower before their outdoor counterparts, the exact time depending on the interior temperature and the plant's blooming stage when cut, among other factors.

Some gardeners achieve good results simply by putting the ends of cut branches in a pail of water and placing it where the branches will get moderate light (but not direct sun). Others recommend a preliminary

Corylopsis makes a good candidate for indoor forcing.

In the Home Garden

Clivia miniata could not be easier to grow and maintain. Camellias, however, are more challenging. Yet their beauty and winter bloom time make them worth the effort required for the northern gardener. Fortunately, new cultivars are always being introduced, some with increased hardiness.

Favorite candidates for late-winter forcing are quince, forsythia, and cherries. In addition to these, suitable plants include winter jasmine (Jasminum nudiflorum), *cornelian cherry dogwood* (Cornus mas), *Japanese cornel dogwood* (Cornus officinalis), *winterhazel* (Corylopsis), *Korean rhododendron* (R. mucronulatum), *and white forsythia* (Abeliophyllum distichum).

Best results are usually obtained with plants nearing their outdoor blooming time. At least six weeks of cold weather are required before dormancy can be broken with good results.

Plants mentioned above that are not listed here are discussed in detail in specific garden sections.

ABELIOPHYLLUM DISTICHUM
White Forsythia, or Korean Abelialeaf
Oleaceae
Korea
Deciduous shrub. White flowers appear before foliage in early spring. Pest free. Prune after flowering, cutting back near ground to rejuvenate. Propagation: softwood cuttings. Size: 3'–5' tall, equal spread. Zones 5–8. Soil: pH adaptable. Sun to light shade.

Camellia japonica 'Drama Girl'

CAMELLIA JAPONICA
Japanese Camellia
Theaceae
China, Japan
Shrub. Handsome evergreen foliage. Exquisite red, pink, white, or variegated blossoms. Winter blooming. Prune after flowering. Propagation: seed and summer cuttings. Innumerable cultivars. Size: 2'–10' tall, 1'–5' spread. Soil: acid, moist, well drained, high organic. Indoors: some sun

in winter. Outdoors: partial shade. Outdoors: zones 7–9, where it can grow much larger.

Camellia japonica 'Amity Wilson'

CLIVIA MINIATA
Kaffir Lily
Amaryllidaceae
South Africa
Tender perennial grown as a houseplant. Large, orange trusses of lilylike flowers in February. Broad, straplike, glossy foliage. Variety flava is yellow. Propagation: seed, division. Cultivars available. Size: 2' tall, 3' spread. Soil: good potting. Moderate light. Outdoors: zones 9–10.

Gardening Basics

Soils, Amendments, and Bed Preparation

Good garden soils hold moisture, have adequate air spaces, and provide the nutrients that plants need. Sandy soils have adequate air spaces, but do not hold moisture well. Clay soils are heavy and will hold moisture, but air spaces are not large enough. A combination of the two soil types is better than either one, but something more is needed in any case: humus. Adding humus is the universal recommendation for improving all soil types.

Humus is organic matter—partially decayed animal and vegetable material—that when added to your soil will do wonders for the health and vigor of your plants. It lightens heavy soil, thus creating air spaces and improving drainage. It adds bulk and texture to sandy soil, holding many times its weight in water or nutrient-laden solutions and giving them up as needed to the plant roots. Just as important, humus fosters an increase in the activity of soil microorganisms that convert materials into forms that plants can use. Earthworms, those more visible engines of beneficial activity, also thrive in soil that is high in humus.

Examples of humus include peat moss, compost, manure, and leaf mold. Many authorities recommend laying down as much as 4"–6" of humus and working it into the soil when preparing beds for planting. Since organic material eventually becomes carbon dioxide or carbonic acid, it gradually leaves the soil and therefore should be replenished regularly.

Mulch

Mulch is a material spread over the soil under plants that provides many benefits to the plants. Mulch keeps down weeds, preserves moisture in the soil, maintains more even temperature for plant roots, and allows rain to better penetrate the soil. It also keeps mud from spattering on low-growing plants and provides a dark background for your garden. Lastly, mulch contributes organic material to the soil as it decomposes. Mulch should be lightweight and porous to allow water and air to the roots of the plants. It is spread over the soil to a depth of one to three inches and should not pack down or form a crust. Suitable mulches are ground pine bark, pine needles, or chopped oak leaves (all good for

Fallen branches and brush on the estate are ground up and stored in a pile. Once a temperature of 140°–160°F has been maintained for three to six months, the material can be used as a mulch.

Foliage is an important indicator of a plant's general health.

acid-loving plants); chopped roots; and wood chippings. Your local nursery can provide information on the types of mulch available in your region that are suitable for the plants you wish to grow.

At Winterthur, horticulturists practice a conservation measure called mulch-mowing. In the fall when herbaceous layers are beginning to die down and leaves have fallen, in a single operation they cut down the material, chop it into a fine, leaf-litter mulch, and allow it to fall back or blow it to where it is wanted. Home owners can adopt this conservation technique by using a mower with a "mulching kit" or a mulch-mowing deck, sometimes called recycling mowers. Handheld leaf vacuums will also chop up fallen leaves to produce a fine organic material. This material can be used either as a mulch or to make leaf mold, or it can be added to a compost pile.

Acid and Alkaline Soils

The pH scale is a convenient way of describing the acidity or alkalinity of soils. A soil pH of 7 is neutral; numbers below 7 indicate acid conditions, whereas those above 7 indicate alkaline situations. You can test your soil either by using a soil test kit or a pH meter, available from garden centers or catalogues, or by taking a soil sample to a reliable soil testing laboratory.

Many of the plants in this book require an acid soil (pH below 7). Rhododendrons and azaleas, for example, grow best in soil whose pH is between 4.5 and 6.0. Soil under pines and oaks is naturally acidic and offers many other advantages to acid-loving plants. Plants requiring somewhat less acidic soils will prosper in a soil pH of 5.0 to 6.5. If a soil test indicates the need to acidify the soil, you can add garden sulfur, ammonium sulfate, ferrous sulfate, aluminum sulfate, peat moss, or acid-producing fertilizers. If soil is too acidic, adding lime (calcium carbonate) is recommended.

Winterthur maintains an active volunteer and internship program. Here, horticulture supervisor David Birk gives pruning tips to summer interns.

Fertilizers

The principal elements found in fertilizers are nitrogen, which promotes lush growth and healthy green foliage color (it is also relatively easily leached out of the soil); phosphorus, which promotes flower and seed development and root growth; and potassium, which promotes strong stems and good root development. These three ingredients are stated in that order as percentages on fertilizer packaging (known as an NPK ratio). A bag that displays a ratio of 10-10-10 is a good all-purpose fertilizer. Secondary elements (calcium, magnesium, and sulfur) and so-called trace elements (boron, chlorine, copper, iron, manganese, molybdenum, zinc, and others), which are needed by plants and sometimes added to commercial fertilizers, are usually present in soils in sufficient quantities, especially those that are organically enriched.

Slow-release fertilizers will provide a slow, continual source of nutrients to your plants. Organic fertilizers, including bone meal, blood meal, fish meal, urea, and wood ashes, are naturally slow-releasing and add organic matter to soil as well. Fertilizers specially formulated for rhododendrons, azaleas, hollies, and other ericaceous plants are safe and effective. For other situations, liquid fertilizers (crystals that are dissolved in water) have the potential to give a quick boost to your plants. These fertilizers are a good way to help along a transplant or new planting, when regular fertilizer might be too harsh for tender roots. Liquid fertilizers are also useful for container plants, spring bulbs gathering nourishment during the short time their foliage is visible, iris ready to bloom, or anything that you want to give some "TLC." For water lilies and other water-grown plants, special aquatic plant tablets should be used.

Integrated Pest Management

Winterthur practices Integrated Pest Management, or IPM, an environmentally responsible approach to pest control. IPM requires selecting disease-resistant plants; meeting their cultural needs; knowing the life cycle of any pests; understanding beneficial insects that are predators of the pests; setting a reasonable limit of damage to be tolerated; and using the least toxic chemicals possible. Careful monitoring and good record keeping are important parts of the program. More

information about IPM for the home gardener is available from the web site of the USDA's Cooperative State Research, Education, and Extension Service at http://www.reeusda.gov/ipm/. Various universities also have web sites devoted to regional IPM programs.

When to Plant

In general, planting may be done in the spring after frost is out of the ground. Nurseries and mail-order houses will ship material when appropriate for your hardiness zone. Local nurseries will have material suitable for your area in each season. Container-grown plants (as opposed to bare-root or balled-and-burlapped plants) can be placed in the garden at almost any time during the growing season since their roots are little disturbed by the transition.

Cuttings

Many of the plants in this book are propagated by cuttings. Softwood cuttings are taken during the growing season; hardwood cuttings are taken when the growth has hardened or when the plant is dormant. In simplest terms, this process consists of removing a 4"–5"-long branch tip, stripping off any lower leaves, dipping the cutting in commercial rooting hormone, and placing it in a rooting medium (which will be kept moist), such as vermiculite, sand, perlite, peat, or some mixture of these. The cutting is then placed in a situation where it will get light and have high humidity until roots have formed. Covering with clear plastic bags, misting, and/or bottom heat are sometimes used to improve the success rate. For more information, consult Michael Dirr's *Manual of Woody Landscape Plants* or Donald Wyman's *Gardening Encyclopedia* (see Suggested Reading, page 172).

Record Keeping

H. F. du Pont, the consummate note-taker, taught us the many advantages to be gained by good record keeping.

Like most devotees, I like to visit my garden each day and have found that recording my thoughts later on a personal computer is most convenient and helpful. In a chronological log I list such information as dates of starting seeds or cuttings and setting out summer bulbs, their subsequent bloom times, and spraying and fertilizing schedules and results. I also have separate sections that note suggestions for the following year; combinations that I like; vases that go well with certain flowers; and any new, environmentally safe ways to deal with pests. An especially useful section, kept at the beginning of each year's log, lists new plants added that year, with cultivar names; places of purchase; and any cultural information that accompanied them. I add my impressions during the year about how well such new plants are performing. Then I have a record in case I want to duplicate or add to a planting in later years or to refer to it for maintenance suggestions.

Du Pont kept notebooks of all sizes on the garden, including his "Flower Garden Notes" seen here.

H. F. du Pont, the consummate note-taker.

Hardiness Zone Map

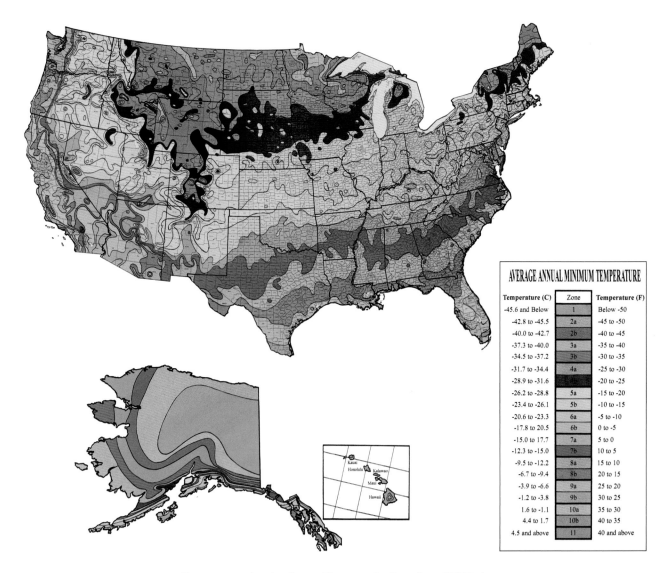

Temperature (C)	Zone	Temperature (F)
AVERAGE ANNUAL MINIMUM TEMPERATURE		
-45.6 and Below	1	Below -50
-42.8 to -45.5	2a	-45 to -50
-40.0 to -42.7	2b	-40 to -45
-37.3 to -40.0	3a	-35 to -40
-34.5 to -37.2	3b	-30 to -35
-31.7 to -34.4	4a	-25 to -30
-28.9 to -31.6		-20 to -25
-26.2 to -28.8	5a	-15 to -20
-23.4 to -26.1	5b	-10 to -15
-20.6 to -23.3	6a	-5 to -10
-17.8 to 20.5	6b	0 to -5
-15.0 to 17.7	7a	5 to 0
-12.3 to -15.0	7b	10 to 5
-9.5 to -12.2	8a	15 to 10
-6.7 to -9.4	8b	20 to 15
-3.9 to -6.6	9a	25 to 20
-1.2 to -3.8	9b	30 to 25
1.6 to -1.1	10a	35 to 30
4.4 to 1.7	10b	40 to 35
4.5 and above	11	40 and above

Courtesy, Agriculture Research Service, USDA

Glossary

bract a modified leaf below a flower

bulb an underground storage organ consisting of modified leaves

bulbil a small bulb arising around the parent bulb; when detached, it will form a new plant

bulblet a small bulb arising in a leaf axil; when detached, it will form new plant

calyx the sepals as a group, directly below petals

clone vegetatively produced progeny of a plant

corm a bulblike underground swollen stem of a plant

cormel a small corm formed at base of parent corm; when detached, it will form a new plant

corolla the petals as a group

corona tubular structure on inner side of petals, such as the trumpet of a daffodil

corymb flat-topped inflorescence in which flowers are held on stems of different lengths

cultivar a named plant, vegetatively produced (a named clone)

cv. abbreviation for cultivar

dioecious male and female flowers on separate plants

exfoliating naturally peeling (bark)

fall the outer petals of an iris

habit characteristic form and mode of growth of a plant

hose-in-hose one corolla inside another, appearing to be one blossom inside another

hybrid offspring of two plants of different species or varieties

indicum late-blooming Japanese rhododendron species

inflorescence collection of individual flowers arranged in some specific fashion

offset small bulb or plant produced by parent plant; when separated will form a new plant

palmate having sections radiating from a common point

panicle inflorescence with branching of flowers on pedicels along an axis pedicel the stalk of a flower

raceme inflorescence in which flowers are held on
stalks along an elongated axis

rhizome an underground modified stem, often fleshy

rugose rough, with impressed veins

sbsp. abbreviation for subspecies,
a division of a species

sepal a leaflike division of the calyx (outer covering
of a flower, directly below the petals)

species a group of individuals having common
characteristics, distinct from other groups;
the basic unit of botanical classification

spike inflorescence in which unstalked flowers are
held on an elongated axis

sport a branch with characteristics different from
the rest of the plant; for example, flowers
of a different color

ssp. abbreviation for species (plural)

standard inner petals of an iris flower,
usually held erect

stoloniferous producing underground shoots

subspecies group within a species showing
minor differences

tepal a segment of flower where corolla and calyx
are undifferentiated; as in magnolia

triploid containing three times the usual complement
of chromosomes

tuber swollen rhizome

umbel flat-topped inflorescence in which all flower
stalks arise from a single point

var. abbreviation for variety

variety a subdivision of a species, varying from other
members in a minor way

whorl group of leaves or flowers arising at one level
around the stem

Suggested Reading

Armitage, Allan M.
Herbaceous Perennial Plants:
A Treatise on Their Identification, Culture,
and General Attributes.
2nd ed. Champaign, Ill.: Stipes Publishing, 1997.

Armitage's Manual of Annuals, Biennials,
and Half-Hardy Perennials.
Portland, Ore.: Timber Press, 2001.

Bruce, Harold
Winterthur in Bloom.
New York: Chanticleer Press, 1986.

Cullina, William.
The New England Wildflower Society Guide
to Growing and Propagating Wildflowers
of the United States and Canada.
Boston: Houghton Mifflin, 2000.

Dirr, Michael A.
Dirr's Hardy Tree and Shrubs:
An Illustrated Encyclopedia.
Portland, Ore.: Timber Press, 1998.

Manual of Woody Landscape Plants:
Their Identification, Ornamental Characteristics,
Culture, Propagation, and Uses.
5th ed. Champaign, Ill.: Stipes Publishing, 1998.

Fiala, Fr. John L.
Lilacs, the Genus Syringa.
Portland, Ore.: Timber Press, 1988.

Frederick, William H., Jr.
The Exuberant Garden and the Controlling Hand:
Plant Combinations for North American Gardens.
Boston: Little, Brown, 1992.

Galle, Fred C.
Azaleas.
Rev. ed. Portland, Ore.: Timber Press, 1995.

Greer, Harold E.
Greer's Guidebook to Available Rhododendrons:
Species and Hybrids.
Eugene, Ore.: Offshoot Publications, 1982.

Hay, Roy, and Patrick M. Synge.
The Color Dictionary of Flowers and Plants.
New York: Crown Publishers, 1982.

Hériteau, Jacqueline, and Charles B. Thomas.
Water Gardens.
Boston: Houghton Mifflin, 1994.

Leach, David G.
Rhododendrons of the World
and How to Grow Them.
New York: Charles Scribner's Sons, 1961.

Liberty Hyde Bailey Hortorium Staff.
Hortus Third: A Concise Dictionary of Plants
Cultivated in the United States and Canada.
Rev. ed. New York: Macmillan, 1976.

Lord, Ruth.
Henry F. du Pont and Winterthur:
A Daughter's Portrait.
New Haven: Yale University Press, 1999.

Magnani, Denise, et al.
The Winterthur Garden:
Henry Francis du Pont's Romance with the Land.
New York: Harry N. Abrams in association
with Henry Francis du Pont Winterthur Museum,
1995.

Phillips, Roger, and Martyn Rix.
The Random House Book of Bulbs.
New York: Random House, 1989.

Perennials.
2 vols. New York: Random House, 1991.

Roses.
New York: Random House, 1988.

Shrubs.
New York: Random House, 1989.

Poor, Janet, and Nancy Peterson Brewster.
Shrubs. Vol. 2 of Plants That Merit Attention.
Portland, Ore.: Timber Press, 1996.

Reiley, H. Edward.
Success with Rhododendrons and Azaleas.
Portland, Ore.: Timber Press, 1992.

Sargent, Walter.
The Enjoyment and Use of Color.
New York: Dover Publications, 1964.

Vivian, John.
Building Stone Walls.
Pownal, Vt.: Garden Way Publishing, 1978.

Wyman, Donald.
Wyman's Gardening Encyclopedia.
New York: Macmillan, 1971.

GENERAL SOURCE LIST

Isaacson, Richard T., ed.
Source List of Plants and Seeds.
5th ed. Chanhassen:
University of Minnesota Press, 2000.

Lists plant species and cultivars as well
as nurseries where they may be purchased.
Invaluable for finding unusual plants.
Contact the University of Minnesota Libraries,
Andersen Horticultural Library,
3675 Arboretum Drive,
P.O. Box 39,
Chanhassen, MN 55317.

Plant Index